Praise

How to Live a Good Life

"Amid the pressure of our everyday routines, it's easy to forget what matters most. We yearn for lives with more energy, enthusiasm, and connection—but where to start? The brilliant Jonathan Fields shows us, in this thought-provoking and action-provoking guide. With engaging (and often funny) stories, cutting-edge research, concrete ideas, and examples from Fields' own experience, How to Live a Good Life *will inspire readers to start living their good lives, today."*

— Gretchen Rubin, *New York Times* best-selling author of *The Happiness Project* and *Better Than Before*

"An incredibly wise, compassionate, and clear guide to living the good life. You'll immediately want to give it to your ten-year-younger self and say 'Read this right now!'"

— Neil Pasricha, *New York Times* best-selling author of *The Book of Awesome* and *The Happiness Equation*

"We've all been there: going through life on autopilot, feeling 'fine' but no longer excited about the dreams we once held so close to our hearts. How to Live a Good Life *will dust off those dreams, bringing them out of forgotten places and back into view."*

— Chris Guillebeau, *New York Times* best-selling author of *Born for This* and *The $100 Startup*

"How to Live a Good Life *skillfully pairs potentiality with action. Fields' voice is refreshingly down-to-earth and his enthusiasm is contagious. My 'Good Life' buckets runneth over after reading this book!"*

— Kristen Noel, Editor-in-Chief, *Best Self*

"Fields is shining his spotlight on possibility—not lofty dreams, not success strategies, not motivational techniques—but possibility. *Straightforward, dynamic, and written with the vitality he wants readers to discover in themselves, this book explains how anyone can live a more energetic, joyful, and passionate life."*

— Anna Jedrziewski, *Retailing Insight*

"Fields offers a simple yet powerful lens through which to look at your life and design your days—through connection, contribution, and vitality. His work is not just a wake-up call, it's a road map and a rousing reminder of your gifts."

— Elena Brower, co-author of *Art of Attention*

"This book is a wake-up call to what really matters in life. Jonathan takes you on a journey where you'll pause, reflect, and prioritize what's most important to living a good life and then give you the simple tools to actually go live it."

— Jadah Sellner, author of *Simple Green Smoothies*

How to LIVE a GOOD LiFe

HOW to LIVE a GOOD LIFE

SOULFUL STORIES, SURPRISING SCIENCE, AND PRACTICAL WISDOM

JONATHAN FIELDS

HAY HOUSE, INC.
Carlsbad, California • New York City
London • Sydney • Johannesburg
Vancouver • New Delhi

Published and distributed in the United States by: Hay House, Inc.: www .hayhouse.com® • *Published and distributed in Australia by:* Hay House Australia Pty. Ltd.: www.hayhouse.com.au • *Published and distributed in the United Kingdom by:* Hay House UK, Ltd.: www.hayhouse.co.uk • *Published and distributed in the Republic of South Africa by:* Hay House SA (Pty), Ltd.: www.hayhouse.co.za • *Distributed in Canada by:* Raincoast Books: www.raincoast.com • *Published in India by:*Hay House Publishers India: www.hayhouse.co.in

Cover design: Caroline Winegeart • *Interior design:* Nick C. Welch • *Interior photos/ illustrations:* Winegeart, Caroline Kelso

"The Summer Day" from *House of Light* by Mary Oliver, published by Beacon Press, Boston. Copyright © 1990 by Mary Oliver, used herewith by permission of the Charlotte Sheedy Literary Agency, Inc.

Library of Congress Cataloging-in-Publication Data

Fields, Jonathan, author.
Title: How to live a good life : soulful stories, surprising science, and
  practical wisdom / Jonathan Fields.
Description: 1st Edition. | Carlsbad : Hay House, Inc., 2016.
Identifiers: LCCN 2016020277 | ISBN 9781401948412 (hardback)
Subjects: LCSH: Self-actualization (Psychology) | Success. | Happiness. |
  BISAC: SELF-HELP / General. | SELF-HELP / Personal Growth / Success. |
  SELF-HELP / Personal Growth / Happiness.
Classification: LCC BF637.S4 F54 2016 | DDC 158--dc23 LC record available at
https://lccn.loc.gov/2016020277

Hardcover ISBN: 978-1-4019-4841-2

12 11 10 9 8 7 6 5 4 3
1st edition, October 2016

Printed in the United States of America

To Mom, with love

CONTENTS

Introduction

I'm the son of a hippie-potter mom and a mad-professor dad. I came of age in the '70s and '80s. Growing up, Duran Duran, ripped jeans, big hair, and Frisbee were my religion. Yes, for those who've glanced at the headshot of me on the inside cover, there was a time I had hair. Same cut as Juan Epstein from *Welcome Back, Kotter*, and it was #GLORIOUS! I just missed the '60s free-love thing, but there was still a lot of love in our house.

Under the surface, though, as I'd come to learn, things weren't as I thought. My parents' marriage was coming apart. Over the years, my mom had become less hippie and my dad more academic. They wanted different things; they'd become different people. My mom had always been fiercely creative, possessed by the urge to make stuff. That's something I inherited from her. Clay was her playground. She'd vanish for days into the basement studio, absorbed in the process of throwing slabs into works of art. As my parents drifted apart, though, life got increasingly complicated. Pulled in many directions, my mom spent less and less time lost in the embrace of her basement pottery studio, largely abandoning the consuming devotion to craft that had been her source of solace, inspiration, identity, salvation, and even income for so many years. In my junior year of high school, my sister split for college. Shortly afterward, my dad moved out, leaving my mom and me alone together in a big old house.

My folks had kept most of the emotional fallout of their separation from us, at least in the early days. Now, Mom and I had to figure out a new dance. She kept up the facade of strength for a while. Then, one day, it all came tumbling down.

I came home to find her sitting on the edge of an old mattress flopped on the floor in the middle of her bedroom—hers alone. Her head lay buried in her knees. Her arms clung to her shins. She was crying. I'd seen her angry plenty of times, especially in the years leading up to the divorce. But I'd never seen her sitting quietly, lights off, weeping.

I didn't know what to do. For the moment, I was being called into the role of caregiver. It was my turn to kiss the boo-boo. But, this wound was soul deep. So I did the only thing I knew. I sat next to her and gently wrapped my arm across her back. "What's wrong?" I asked. In a somber silence that seemed to linger interminably, the unease of reversing roles washed through me. I almost hoped she wouldn't answer. Then I wouldn't need to figure out how to respond. My standard fallback to 17-year-old sarcasm wouldn't close this gap.

"I lost it," she whispered. "I went downstairs to the studio today. I sat at the wheel, grabbed some clay, and tried to throw. I kept trying. But I couldn't do it. It's gone." On the surface, the "it" she was talking about was her near-mystical mastery over clay. Just below that, it was the entirety of her being. Her identity as a maker, an artist, a powerful woman, and a creator. Her ability to reconnect with joy, to play, to get lost in a process, to achieve and be recognized, to put money in the bank and food on the table. The "it" that had left her was the very essence of who she believed herself to be. Somehow, at 17, I got that.

I wanted to cry along with her. Instead, I spoke. I'd trained as a gymnast for years, so this metaphor tumbled clumsily out. "You haven't lost it, Mom; you're just rusty. It's like me and gymnastics. You know how I get into great shape for competition during the season, but then during the off-season I kind of fall apart. And when I come back to training camp the week before we start, I'm pretty terrible. It takes me a few weeks to get everything back. But it always comes back. Once it's in you, it's in you. You've been away from it for a while. You haven't lost anything. You're just rusty. It'll take a little time to get it back, but you will."

As she listened, the crying began to ease. Her breathing relaxed and she looked up. "Yeah," she said, "that makes sense." A spark of hope emerged, along with a gentle smile, and she gave me a hug. Later that evening, I heard the clank of the basement door as she made her way back into the studio.

I've often wondered why this moment has stayed with me. It would be years before I realized what had actually happened. What had been revealed to me. And it would be many more years until I gave myself permission to own the possibility that somewhere within me lay the ember of a rough-edged ability to affect others. Both the desire and the potential to create moments, experiences, and things that might inspire a change in state and belief. To incite possibility.

This potential to make a difference is, truth told, something I still grapple with. Owning it feels a little too trippy for my rational brain and a little too forward facing and arrogant for my more introverted, maker self. When my last book was named the number one personal development book of the year by 800-CEO-READ, I was publicly grateful, but privately I recoiled at the label and what I believed it implied, both about me and about the work I was doing in the world. I'm not that guy, I offered quietly to friends. I'm about business, entrepreneurship, language, and creativity. Yet everywhere I've turned there have been signs. You are all those, those same friends would reply, but underneath it all, you're about something bigger: creating vehicles and pathways and moments that allow people to embrace their potential. To connect. To reveal. To see and engage with possibility.

I've come to learn that not owning this part of me out of fear of some kind of external judgment or label—well, that causes its own pain. It keeps me from doing what I'm here to do. Having refused the call for so long (I'm slow; what can I say?), I finally realized it was time to step into it.

That gradual awakening has fueled years of seeking and study and fierce engagement with life. It eventually brought me back to my seat not just as a student, but also as a maker, a mentor, a writer, and a teacher. It's the reason this book exists.

Who Is This Book For?

I wrote this book with one person in mind but soon discovered she was, in fact, the face, the heart, the soul, and the stifled yearning of millions. From the outside looking in, she had so many reasons to be grateful. A confident woman in her middle years, she was building a career, had plenty of friends and shared interests, and put on a great show of health. She knew she was, in so many ways, blessed. But that did little to quell the undercurrent of yearning and her growing sense of stifled potential. Her deeper reality, like that of so many of us, told a different story.

She had given up so much in the name of being an adult and partner; a source of unflagging, always-on strength and wisdom, kindness and understanding, security and surrender. Everything to everyone at all times, except herself.

What had happened to those deep interests and passions, the burning questions, delicious topics, joyful activities, and moments of transcendent awe that had been at the center of her younger life? They had long been relegated to the land of lost socks and somedays. Being lit up ceded the way to being grown-up.

Nobody else saw that she was increasingly uncomfortable in her own skin, but she knew. Standing before her mirror revealed more than clothes could ever hide. It wasn't just about the way she looked; it was about the way she felt. Her health and vitality, her sexual and sensual core, had gone the way of her exercise and former identity. Her friends, numerous as they were, drifted somewhere "out there," wrapped in their own versions of sweet oblivion. Sure, there was the occasional "Let's do lunch" text, but without fail, it would linger unanswered in the digital ether. She had her "people," but having them and being with them were two different things. She was never truly alone but often lonely.

She met each day overwhelmed with a sense of pervasive busyness, and fractured attention. It was as if a swarm of "interested parties" were in control and her job, from the moment she opened her eyes to the moment she lay down to sleep, was not to choose with intention but to mindlessly react to an ever-expanding list of other people's agendas. Punch lists replaced purpose and possibility. Awakening one morning, she thought, *Welcome to my autopilot life.*

Maybe most upsetting was that pervasive sense of untapped potential, as if the "real" her was screaming to get out, to reclaim that lit-up self she used to be or silently yearned to become. She'd give anything to close the gap between the life she knew she was capable of living and the one that met her every morning. And she was gut-tired of answering "busy" and "fine" and "surviving" whenever someone asked, "How are you?" She was desperate to be in a place where she would look up when asked and, with a radiant smile, reply, "So damn good!"

She had flatlined on nearly every level. It was as if she were living that classic lyric from Pink Floyd: she'd become "comfortably numb." For years, she didn't want to own it. Despite her slow descent into what Teddy Roosevelt famously described as "the gray twilight that knows neither victory nor defeat," there was extraordinary good in her life. She knew this. With so much "real" suffering in the world, she had just written off her state of disillusionment, disconnection, and malaise as a "first-world problem" because it was more about elevation than survival. And who was she to complain? Who was she to want more? Framing it this way not only made her feel greedy for wanting more, but gave her a seemingly rational justification for inaction. But there was something else. If she stood in her deeper truth, if she really owned it, she'd also have to own both her role in arriving at that place and her responsibility to do what was necessary to create a different future. And that terrified her, because she had no idea how to bridge the gap between where she was and where she so desperately wanted to be.

Until she finally hit her breaking point.

I wrote this book for her—but then, I'm guessing if you've read this far, there's a good chance she is you. Even if you're a guy. Even if you're just graduating from college. Even if you're starting over a bit further into life. We've all felt what she felt at different moments along the road. We've all been in that place of "fine" and "busy," disconnected from the people, places, and activities that allow us to walk through each day utterly alive. Disconnected from our best selves. We've all felt like a piece of us was dying a little bit every day and we just didn't know how to flip the switch, how to turn our lives back on. And we've all spun the conversation in our heads that justified inaction and complacency. The one that kept us cocooned, safe from the unknown, but also estranged from the possible.

Sadly, we are not alone. In a world where awareness and intention long ago lost the battle to mindless surrender, we're not even the exception. For years, if not decades, we've been living with an undiagnosed condition: Reactive Life Syndrome. Living each day not by choice, but by default. Doing what we can simply to keep up and tread water. It's not about getting ahead, but rather about desperately trying not to fall too far behind. And in the end, it's a losing proposition. The great news is that it's not too late. There is an antidote.

If you're nodding and saying, "That's me. This is what I need. I am ready," then this book will serve as your guide. The community you'll discover around the ideas in the book will help ensure that, maybe for the first time in your life, you'll move from existing to living, and from knowing what to do to actually doing it.

But then, I'm guessing you've heard that line before. And you're wondering, "Really? How is this going to give me back my life? What makes it so different? And who are *you* to tell *me* what to do?"

With your permission, I'll start with that last question.

Who Am *I* to Write *This* Book, and How Is It Different?

My finger hovered over the send button. "Who am I," I wondered, "to propose a book entitled *How to Live a Good Life?*" The arrogance! A middle-aged, married dad from the Upper West Side of Manhattan pontificating on the single most vexing question in all of human history. What do *I* have to say about how to live a good life that hasn't been said or shared a million times before? Funny enough, a large part of my work is helping people and companies who've lost their sense of identity, voice, and meaning answer this very question. *Who am I to have something to say?* As I sat with the question, the words of iconic dancer and choreographer Martha Graham, offered in Agnes de Mille's biography *Martha: The Life and Work of Martha Graham,*[1] settled over me:

> There is vitality, a life force, energy, a quickening that is translated through you into action, and because there is only one of you in all of time, this expression is unique. And if you block it, it will never exist through any other medium and it will be lost. The world will not have it. It is not your business to determine how good it is nor how valuable nor how it compares with other expressions. It is your business to keep it yours clearly and directly, to keep the channel open. You do not even have to believe in yourself or your work. You have to keep yourself open and aware to the urges that motivate you. Keep the channel open. . . .

Adding value to another's life is not about being a guru, a sage, or a wizard. It's not about placing yourself above others, preaching down, or telling anyone to "sit and listen while I save you from the world and yourself." When I look at the astonishing body of wisdom around the pursuit of a good life, from the Stoics to the Buddha, from faith to science and metaphysics to mythology, it's clear to me that there is little, if anything, that's not been studied or said before. There are precious few new ideas. Yet, in the face of this gob-smackingly huge collection of wisdom, much of humanity stumbles along, eternally yearning for a life it knows is possible, but having no idea how to find or create it.

The problem isn't that we don't have the answers. We've had them for thousands of years. It's that the things that work are either engulfed in a vast sea of noise or offered in a way that doesn't land. They're too hard to find and validate, too complicated, too theoretical, too mired in dogma, that war with the reality of our lives.

I'm not here to claim ownership of something profound and new, but rather to help you separate the wheat from the chaff. To identify the big levers, the things that work. And then to share them in a way that preserves their potential but also goes down easy. A way that inspires not just understanding, but action and integration, without the need for blind faith, godlike willpower, or total disruption.

My role has been to live fiercely and study deeply. To walk through each day an eternal student. To wade into Joseph Campbell's disquieting abyss in search of our treasure. Hopefully the way I share my unique understanding and experience will somehow connect with the way you need to hear or see or feel something at this moment. Maybe some small piece will awaken a part of your story in a manner that helps you breathe a little easier, love a little more openly, or live a little more fully. That is my intention in writing this book.

But what about you? All I ask is this: Stay open. Hold on a little less tightly to the safety of a consistent yet failed past and to the perceived sanctity of truths that may or may not have served you and the way you dream of being in the world. As Mark Twain famously offered, "It ain't what you don't know that gets you into trouble. It's what you know for sure that just ain't so."

Where Do the Ideas I'm about to Share Come From?

In the next chapter, I'll offer a simple model that you can use to guide nearly every decision in life, something I call the Good Life Buckets. Where does it come from? In part, from decades of study. Some at the feet of extraordinary thinkers and teachers, from Buddhist lamas to education reformers and grounded-theory researchers to neuroscientists. Other learning comes from thousands of hours and decades of quiet study and contemplation, devouring everything from Thomas Merton to the *Bhagavad Gita* to reams of academic studies and research reports.

Then there's the wisdom that can come only from some 50 years of life. Lessons learned through more than two decades building communities and companies, failing repeatedly and finding the will to step back into the arena until I got it right. Years teaching everything from yoga to entrepreneurship to thousands of students from around the world, speaking on stages large and small, working with everyone from soccer moms to CEOs and movie stars to moguls, leading retreats, writing books, and lecturing at universities. But without question, my deepest, most humbling growth has come from being a dad and a husband, and from my daily practice, one that cultivates a deepening stillness and continues to awaken me to the life-affirming truth of my own impermanence and the urgency that comes from accepting that on a day unknown to me, I and all those I love will be gone. Each of these experiences has shaped what Martha Graham would call my "unique" expression of life. My quickening. My channel. And they've all found an outlet in the venture that now commands a good part of my vocation, Good Life Project®.

In January 2012, I began to write what had normally been an annual essay that inventoried and reflected on the year behind and set intentions for the year to come. That document rapidly grew into a 34-page Warren Buffet–style annual report that I published and shared on my blog. On the final two pages, entitled "2012 Reimagined," I shared a story, and an invitation:

> "What inspires you?"
>
> That's what an audience member asked during my keynote at a conference last summer.
>
> Little did she know, I had something hidden . . . something the audience couldn't see . . . a little piece of paper resting on the monitor next to my notes . . .
>
> It was there to remind me what really mattered. I could crash and burn on stage, but this piece of paper would make it all okay.

It was a heart. Drawn for me by my 10-year old daughter before I left. No matter how my keynote went, she'd still be there to place her hands on my cheeks when I walked in the door and share a few butterfly kisses and a hug that said, "You're everything I need."

I held up the heart in response to the question and said, "This. My daughter," then explained what it was. Standing there, with the piece of paper raised high in the air before 500 people, I nearly burst into tears. So did many in the audience.

That piece of paper with the hastily drawn heart comes with me when I travel. If I'm on stage, it's there with me. But there was more. An invitation bundled with an announcement. Ten ideas, a different approach to building not just a living, but a life. And a new venture, one that would take my (until then) very personal exploration of life well lived and turn it far more public than I'd ever planned.

What if I shared my quest, I thought. Sitting down with teachers, known and unknown, filming and recording the conversations, then not only learning but offering these people and ideas up to the world. What if I made it my full-time pursuit to find, learn from, and share people with pieces of the puzzle? People like the ephemerally wise and wickedly funny Brené Brown. People like polio survivor and education revolutionary Sir Ken Robinson. People like Shambhala Buddhist lama Sakyong Mipham Rinpoche, a fiftysomething Tibetan lama whose name literally translates to "Earth Protector." People like iconic graphic designer Milton Glaser, who, when I sat down with him at the age of 85 remained stunningly prolific, deeply committed, creating, teaching, and playing with his wife of some 60 years. People like acclaimed illustrator Lisa Congdon, who stumbled into art in her 30s and made it her life. Or famed behavioral economist and psychologist Dan Ariely, whose fascination with human nature and subsequent vocation were triggered by a three-year stint as a patient in an Israeli burn ward at the age of 18. What if I could travel the world, visit with these beacons of life-earned wisdom and light, learn at their feet, integrate what I learned with my own experience of life, my own unique view, voice, and channel, and then share it all with the world?

With that, Good Life Project® was born. And without intention, the very early seeds of this book were planted. Now years into this quest, those seeds of an idea that began as a deep yearning to learn and share have grown into a media and education venture with a global community, an acclaimed web series and podcast with hundreds of thousands of listeners and viewers in more than 150 countries. We've also grown a catalog of courses, gatherings, events, and even an annual celebration, Camp GLP, where "GLeePers" from all over the world converge on a summer camp for three and a half days of pure magic.

Along the way, the incredible access to extraordinary minds and gorgeous souls began to cross-pollinate with my own experiences, and something profound began to emerge, a simple model I began to call the Good Life Buckets. This easy-to-digest framework offers a way to look at the life you're living, quickly and easily assess what's working and what's not, and instantly know where to focus your energy to make things better; then it tells you what to do. I began to share the Good Life Buckets with increasingly large groups and within our courses and gatherings. The response took my breath away.

Mel Charbonneau, a married mother of two young kids and cofounder of the emerging women's movement Fellow Flowers, was one of the first to learn about the buckets. In the middle of one of our intensive seven-month training programs, she shared some great news. She was pregnant with her third child. And, much to my surprise, the Good Life Buckets played a major role in both her decision to have another child and how she would completely reconfigure her life to continue to flourish as a mom and an entrepreneur and live a great life. In her words:

> Having another child was a big deal. I'm in major start-up mode with my business, giving it a ton of my time, creativity, and energy. And I already have two little girls, ages 7 and 4, who get all my love and attention

when I'm not in biz mode. My husband and I had just figured out our groove with family and business when I realized something big—I really wanted to have another baby. How do you have that conversation?

How do you discuss those big pieces of your life that will have to once again get reacclimatized? Enter the buckets. When I returned home from Costa Rica, it was like I had a whole new dialogue to share with my husband, which helped guide our decision and reaffirm what was most important to us. It gave us context for questions and conversation. . . . It actually became really good motivation to pause, prioritize, and let go of a few things. For our marriage, it brought us closer because connection (family relationships) is the MOST important part of our life, and now our goal is to make a contribution and vitality support plan and nurture that, leaving room for the fun, chaos, and adventures of life.

Charbonneau is just one of so many examples. As more people learned about the Good Life Buckets, I noticed something wonderful. They began speaking in "the language" of the buckets—"I'm feeling like this one bucket needs filling today"—and using it to guide their decisions, big and small. The outcomes were better than I ever imagined, and with its application in the real world, I've been able to refine the model. This book is your window into this seemingly simple yet transformational tool, explaining how you can tap the buckets to guide your decisions and actions in the quest to live a great life.

Let's Get Your Good Life Going!

It's time to set in motion your personal Good Life Project. To discover a new way to get from where you are now to where you know in your bones you're capable of being.

Before we dive in, one last thought: This book is your road map. The approach, ideas, and many invitations to act, to play, to connect, and to embody what you're learning on a daily basis will serve as a hybrid good-life manifesto and a practical yet powerful guide. One that allows you to ease into a process of awakening and becoming in a way that feels right to you.

At the same time, the real magic happens when you put down the book and start doing the work. So I've created a set of additional resources not only to ensure you stay supported, feel inspired, and are held while you're "doing" the book, but also to help you carry the learning and doing into the rest of your life.

Throughout the book, you'll see references to a web page called goodlifeproject.com/bookinsider. Here, I'll share a wide range of free resources, links, downloadable files, worksheets, guided audio, and more, all in one place. You'll also find an invitation to join our beautiful, supportive, and private Good Life Project online community, crafted around an ethos of generosity, compassion, nonjudgment, and elevation. There you'll find a place to share your experiences, ask questions, find accountability partners and support, and more. Oh, and don't be surprised if you also end up making a bunch of friends along the way. Our "GLeePer" family has been known to be a pretty friendly lot!

Onward then—to the buckets we go!

Think of your life as three buckets.

The first bucket is called Vitality, and it's about the state of your mind and body. The second is Connection; this one is about relationships. The third, Contribution, is about how you contribute to the world.

The fuller your buckets, the better your life. When all simultaneously bubble over, life soars. That's what we're aiming for. But the flip side is also true. If any single bucket runs dry, you feel pain. If two go empty, a world of hurt awaits. If all three bottom out, you don't have a life. Figuratively and, in short order, literally.

There are likely hundreds if not thousands of ways to fill your Good Life Buckets. But, as promised, this simple framework and book are about making your life easier. For all three buckets, we'll keep our focus on a very small number of what I call bucket-filling "big levers." These are the little things that will fill your buckets most powerfully. In the chapters that follow, you'll discover 10 ways to fill each bucket.

Before we get there, let's go a bit deeper into each bucket. Then we'll take a quick snapshot that will tell you how full each of *your* buckets is right now (don't worry, no judgments). After that, you'll learn the three "laws of the buckets." That'll give you everything you need to start your own Good Life Project and dive into the chapters that follow.

Let's start with your Vitality Bucket.

Your Vitality Bucket

"None of the other stuff is going to work if the animal that you live in is just a broke-down mess." — Elizabeth Gilbert

If you don't have your health, we've all heard, you don't have anything. You can't buy your way out of a tumor. Or depression. Or illness. Or pain. You can't feel alive, happy, and joyful when your body is abandoning you. And you can't drink in all that life has to offer when your body is limited in its capabilities. Not only that, but a vital body is the vessel for that three-pound bundle of consciousness called your brain, the thing that processes whether you're living a good life or not. The thing that feels and chooses, that controls your organs, systems, and movements. There is a powerful feedback loop between your mind and body.

What exactly is vitality, then? For our purposes, vitality is an optimal state of body and mind. When you think about the state of your body and mindset, you want to feel:

- Energized
- Fit, strong, and flexible enough to participate in life
- As free from pain, disease, and disability as possible
- Aware of and capable of being in the moment
- Optimistic about the future and what it holds
- Peaceful and calm, able to dissipate stress
- Able to bounce back from adversity
- Immersed in a process of growth
- Grateful for what's right in life
- Fueled by a sense of meaning
- Happy

Notice that vitality isn't just about our bodies. It's about our minds. Why is that? Because, in truth, there is no distinction. Your mind and body serve as seamless feedback mechanisms, chemically and electrically. They are so hopelessly intertwined that it's silly to speak of them as separate. The state of your body—its health, strength, disease, ability, or disability —has a profound effect on your mind. If your body is in pain, so is your brain. We get that. Less intuitive, though, is that if your mind is in pain, so is your body. Depression, anxiety, sadness, stress, and heartbreak all create real, measurable physical symptoms in our bodies, ranging from pain to inflammation and disease. By the same token, joy, love, belonging, meaning, peace, and ease create a cascade of positive effects that we feel equally. When we head into the daily explorations to fill your Vitality Bucket, we'll explore things that elevate both mind and body.

Okay, let's head on over to your Connection Bucket.

Your Connection Bucket

"There is nothing I would not do for those who are really my friends. I have no notion of loving people by halves, it is not my nature." — Jane Austen, Northanger Abbey

Our Connection Bucket is about nourishing relationships. It's about intimate partners, family, close friends, colleagues, coconspirators, and like-minded community. It's about love and lust, passion and compassion, resonance and belonging. It's also about how well we know and relate to ourselves. And for some, it's also about our relationship with the experience of something greater than ourselves, whether we define that as God, source, spirit, consciousness, nature, the divine, field, or anything else.

We are innately social beasts, born to be with others. When we're with the right others, in the right way, magic happens. We come alive and our world, our capacity to flourish and grow and engage with life and joy, expands. When we're with the wrong people, in the wrong way, or isolated from the right people, everything shrinks. Our ability to drink in all life has to offer crumbles. When we're completely alone, isolated from humanity, we first lose our minds, then wither and die. Yes, even the rare professed diehard mega-introverts among us.

In order to fill our Connection Buckets, we need to find and be with "our people." Those we can love and those who'll love us back. Those we can befriend and play and laugh with. Those who will serve as a source of acceptance, allegiance, and belonging. In other words, those who just plain get us.

When we think about the relationships in our lives, we want to feel like:

- We give love and receive love, without condition
- We belong—we're seen, understood, and embraced by friends with shared values, interests, and aspirations (and sometimes culture)
- We are connected to something bigger than ourselves, be it natural or ethereal

How do you cultivate these connections and relationships and the luscious, bucket-filling feelings that ride along with them? You'll discover 10 powerful ways in our Connection Bucket daily explorations.

That brings us to the final bucket.

Your Contribution Bucket

"Imagine immensities. Pick yourself up from rejection and plow ahead. Don't compromise. Start now. Start now, every single day." — Debbie Millman

Your Contribution Bucket is about how you bring your gifts to the world. It's the answer to the poet Mary Oliver's gorgeous question, "Tell, me, what is it you plan to do with your one wild and precious life?"

It's about contributing to the world, even if that world is a single person, in a way that is meaningful, in a way that matters and allows you to feel like you matter. It's about that deep knowing that you're doing the thing you're here to do. There's a sense of calling that's pulling you from ahead, rather than pushing you from behind. It's about being lit up along the way, absorbed in that semi-trance state beyond emotion, where time ceases to exist and you feel like you're channeling pure consciousness. It's about feeling like you're accessing your full potential, your strengths, your gifts, the deepest parts of your humanity, leaving nothing unrealized or untapped. You are fully expressed, seen, and heard.

To fill our Contribution Buckets, we need to cultivate these feelings. How? As with our Vitality and Connection Buckets, the universe of possible contributors is large. We'll focus on 10 big filling levers for our Contribution Buckets in the daily explorations that follow.

That brings us to the Three Laws of the Buckets.

The Three Laws of the Buckets

Bucket Law #1: The buckets leak.

In the early days, our buckets are new and shiny. No dents or cracks, no rust or tarnish. But over time they get a bit dinged, the paint wears thin, and the seams that held together so tightly begin to separate just a bit. Then they begin to leak. Not a ton, but enough so that we can't just fill them once and know they'll stay topped off for life. Left alone, our buckets eventually run dry. And so does life. Our job, then, is to keep circling around, filling them as needed, and never ignoring any one long enough for it to run dry.

Bucket Law #2: Your emptiest bucket will drag the others down with it.

Intuitively we know this. Let our Vitality Buckets run dry and it'll be impossible to contribute anywhere near the level of our true potential or sustain relationships in a way that fills our Connection Buckets effectively. Let our Connection Buckets run dry and it becomes brutally hard to muster the energy needed to do the things that fill our Vitality and Contribution Buckets. Let our Contribution Buckets run dry, spending all our energies on things that devour our time but empty our souls, and we'll have trouble finding the reserves needed to cultivate rewarding relationships and a vital mind and body. All the buckets are connected. We cannot fill any one to its full capacity unless the others fill along with it. Put another way, we can abandon one in the name of filling the others for only so long, before we need to circle back and do all our buckets right.

Bucket Law #3: The buckets never lie.

We often bring a certain amount of well-intended delusion to the assessment of how full or empty our buckets are. We like to think they're fuller and easier to fill than they are. Think what you want, but the buckets don't lie. If you let one run dry, all the delusion and excuse in the world won't help. Empty is empty. You can't think it full. Be optimistic about the future but honest about the present.

Now we have a new tool to guide our decisions and actions. And we've learned a simple set of rules to help get us on our way. It's great new information. But as author and visionary thinker Derek Sivers offers, "If information was the answer, then we'd all be billionaires with perfect abs." Knowledge is meaningless without action. It's time to move from knowing to doing, to start filling our Good Life Buckets!

How to Fill Your Good Life Buckets

The Good Life Buckets offer a simple framework that is easy to understand. It's intuitive, straightforward, and readily remembered. You may even find yourself, at any given moment, asking, "Which bucket needs filling right now?" That's awesome. This simple question gives you so much power. It tells you immediately where to focus your energy to build your best moment, your best day, and, over time, your best life.

That said, I want to make it as easy as possible to not only learn but take action on what you're learning and get started right away. The rest of this chapter will set you up to do just that. Here are the steps:

- Take your 60-second snapshot
- Draft your team
- Join our virtual family
- Choose your path
- Rock it out!

Let's start with your snapshot.

Take Your 60-Second Snapshot

Your 60-second snapshot tells you how full or empty each of your buckets is right now. It gives you a starting point that helps you decide which bucket to start filling first, and it provides a reference point for comparing future snapshots and tracking progress over time. To complete your 60-second snapshot, answer these three questions:

- *For your Vitality Bucket, "At this moment in time,* how satisfied am I with my current level of physical ability, energy, appearance, and well-being, my ability to weather adversity, and my capacity to feel calm, aware, present, in charge, optimistic, and joyful?"

- *For your Connection Bucket, "At this moment in time,* how satisfied am I with the depth and quality of my loving relationships, friendships, and sense of genuine belonging?"

- *For your Contribution Bucket, "At this moment in time,* how satisfied am I with the level of meaning that I feel from the way I'm bringing my gifts to the world?"

For each of these questions, assign a number from 0 to 10, 0 being terribly unsatisfied and 10 being the most satisfied possible. Then write down your answer to this question: "What is making this the number I chose?" For example, what is making my level of energy or my love or sense of meaning a two?" Finally, ask yourself what a 10 would look and feel like, then write that down.

To make this easier to complete and to enable you to take new snapshots over time, so you can both track your progress and reassess where to focus your bucket-filling energies, I've created a free, downloadable 60-Second Snapshot Worksheet for you. Or, if you want to create the most powerful snapshot possible, check out the free Snapshot360™ online quiz. It'll walk you through a series of detailed questions that will give a far more thorough snapshot than can be created with the 60-second overview. The 60-second worksheet and online quiz are available at goodlifeproject.com/bookinsider.

Remember, the snapshot is just a freeze-frame. It is not a judgment about where we've been or how we got here. Our job, now, is not to judge what brought us to this place, but to own where we are and use this new set of tools to make different decisions, take different actions, and plot a course to the best life we're capable of living.

Draft Your Good Life Project Team

"If you want to go fast, travel alone. If you want to go far, travel together." — *African proverb*

If we go it alone, our chances of sticking with almost anything are pretty awful. This is especially true of things we may not perceive as enjoyable or things that require a certain amount of skill before they become fun. These things often require a solid chunk of willpower, especially in the early days.

What may be more surprising, though, is that this also applies to things we love to do. Think about it. You take a yoga class or an art class and love it. You want to do more, so you start to do it three times a week. Then life happens. You have to travel, or maybe you get a cold, you have a big, crazy deadline, or your demanding relatives hit town and want to play with you all day, every day. Your routine goes out the window, and despite how much you were loving it, you struggle to get back into it. The longer it takes, the more shame you feel and the more you fear that first day back. Eventually you just pretend the whole thing never happened. Must've been a dream.

This is one of the reasons so many of us, well intended and with good information, still fail at doing things we not only hold dear but really enjoy. There is no magic to awesome outcomes. Whether we're looking to build a great career, a great relationship, great health, or a great life, it's all about consistent action over time. It's about coming back after things blow up, over and over and over. Because they will, and we'll need a way to reclaim our daily routine. Books are great for learning, but they're terrible for action, accountability, and celebration. We can't hug a page or get a check-in from a footnote.

The single most powerful driver of action and success is social support. Put another way, we need people to keep us accountable to even the most enjoyable actions in life. And not just any people; we want people who are along for the ride, on the same great adventure as us. People who get what we're doing because they're doing it, too. Together we provide love, support, accountability, celebration, insight, and belonging.

Take a few minutes and think about who else might want to join you in this adventure. Who else could really use a good life intervention right now? Who would you love to play with as you co-create your big, beautiful lives? See if you can think of at least two others, then reach out to them and tell them what you're about to do. Invite them to be on your own Team Good Life and offer to be on theirs.

If only one person comes to mind, start with that person. One is better than none. But see if you can line up at least two. Why? Because at any given time, one of your people may be unavailable. Having three (five at most) on your Team Good Life makes it much more likely that at least two of you will be there to keep your personal Good Life Project on track. If you can find those potential teammates where you are, fantastic. If not, as I said earlier, we've created a global virtual community to help you out.

Join Our Virtual Family

If it's easy to find people to be on your Team Good Life in your community, that's great. I'd also love to invite you to become a member of our private Good Life Project online community at GoodLifeProject.com/community. There, you'll discover a warm and supportive virtual family and benefit from the connection, celebration, friendship and accountability that fuels consistent action and lifechanging outcomes.

Now you have a good sense of your starting point and understand which buckets are most in need of filling. You have your people to help support you and celebrate along with you. That leaves us with one final question.

What is the best way to "do" the rest of this book?

The chapters that follow are divided into three sections. The first focuses on filling your Vitality Bucket. The next is about filling your Connection Bucket. The last one discusses filling your Contribution Bucket. Within each section, you'll find 10 short and sweet chapters. These are your daily explorations. Each focuses on a single bucket-filling idea and then offers a daily exploration. Some explorations are one-time actions or things to think about. Others are practices to begin and then deepen over time.

What's the best way to move through the sections and chapters? Here are two suggestions. Choose the one that feels most right to you.

Two Paths: Deep Dive or 30-Day Challenge

Path #1: The Bucket-by-Bucket Deep Dive

This approach works well when our snapshot shows that one specific bucket is in need of a lot more love than the other two. If that's you, flip to the section that covers your emptiest bucket. You'll find 10 chapters, each with a single idea and daily exploration designed to help you refill that particular bucket a bit more. Read one chapter a day, then do the daily exploration at the end of each chapter.

For example, if your Connection Bucket is low, head over to the section entitled Fill Your Connection Bucket and do a deep dive. Work through the chapters, one per day, if that fits into your life, or on any other schedule that honors your life's demands but also keeps you accountable and engaged. Once done, move onto the next-emptiest bucket and do the same until you've eventually completed your deep dive into each bucket.

In the final chapter of the book I'll talk more about how to keep the growth going after this deep dive.

Path #2: The 30-Day Good Life Bucket Challenge

If your snapshot showed that all of your buckets were in need of love and there wasn't a clear "winner," a fun alternative to the bucket-by-bucket deep dive is the 30-day challenge.

Here's how it works. For the next 30 days, read one chapter a day and complete the daily exploration at the end of that chapter.

On Day 1, read and do the first chapter under Vitality. On Day 2, read and do the first chapter under Connection. On Day 3, read and do the first chapter under Contribution. Then keep circling through the buckets every day for 30 days until you reach the end.

This is, no doubt, a pretty fierce approach, but it is incredibly powerful to commit to something for 30 days. It's a short enough amount of time to keep your commitment, but also long enough to experience a real shift in the way you experience your life.

Let's Make It Happen

Annie Dillard wrote, "A good life is made of a series of good days, starting with today." Our job is not so much to go from here to there, but to wake up. To own our current reality. To see it. Feel it. Accept it. Then take action to start living the life we dream of living. One breath, one step, one day at a time. Not later. Not tomorrow. But today. Right now.

Grab my hand.

Everything will be okay.

We'll do it together.

DAY 1

WAKE UP

Take One—Autopilot and Reactive

It's 6:30 A.M. The sound of a loud, buzzing alarm on your iPhone gets you to crack open your eyes. You fumble for the device and turn it off. For all intents and purposes, that is the last intentional act you'll take until you lay your head down to sleep some 16 hours later. Every moment in between will be spent reacting to other people's plans for your day. Before getting out of bed or even acknowledging anyone sharing it, you check your e-mail to see who will be setting your agenda, based on their needs, followed by Facebook, Twitter, Instagram, Snapchat, and voice mail. Ten seconds in, and already you've lost control over how you spend your day.

By the time you leave the house, your to-do list exceeds the day's capacity and you're living in a future set by someone else's agenda. Every step along the way, your mind is somewhere else. Reacting to prompts, things other people tell you are important without ever stopping to ask whether they matter to you. It's gorgeous out, but you don't notice. Your kid, partner, lover, or parent smells great, terrible, or fruity, but you don't pick it up. You stop for a coffee. Waiting in line, you check again. And it's not just you. All heads are buried up their collective apps. A twentysomething woman sits at a corner table sketching, and her work is beautiful. Nobody sees it. You drive to work and spend the next nine hours responding to e-mail in real time, checking to-dos off your list, rifling through Facebook, Twitter, and Snapchat again, and again, and again. Checking voice mail and calling people back. Check, check, check. By the time you land home, you've checked a lot of boxes. You've been busy, so busy, you really must be important. You've gotten so much done. But you can't remember a thing you've accomplished. You feel like your checklist for tomorrow is already longer than what you started with today. And very little of it is meaningfully connected to anything you care about. Your only intention is to survive, and if that means embracing what was good in your day and proactively creating your tomorrow, you've failed mightily.

Welcome to your autopilot reactive life. If you're like the average person, you will check your smartphone more than 150 times. You'll lose more than three hours in the process and end up on Facebook without even thinking about it.[2]

Take Two—Aware and Intentional

7:30 A.M. You awaken to the sound of One Republic's "Good Life," which you've chosen as the first track on your wake-up Spotify playlist because it makes you smile. You listen for a minute with your eyes closed. Placing both hands over your heart, eyes still closed, you set an intention for the day, to approach every interaction from a place of loving-kindness and mutual benefit. Still in a semi-alert state, you rise into a sitting position in bed as your playlist rolls into a 15-minute guided meditation. Your mind feels calm and focused. You ease into the shower, where you notice how good the warm, pulsing water feels on your back. Drying off, you slide back to the bedroom and hit PLAY. Marvin Gaye takes over. You want to dance, but instead you dress and make breakfast. Sitting over coffee, for the first time, you check your e-mail, but only to scan and ensure there is no true emergency that requires an immediate response, remembering that someone else's procrastination or engineered neurosis is not your emergency. You do not reply or delete or file anything. You close your device and open your Moleskine to a simple, lined page where last night you wrote out the single most important thing that must be accomplished today. The one that will be the biggest lever in the area of deepest meaning. You then revisit the two supporting actions written below and confirm all three are still today's priorities.

You head to work, and your phone remains tucked away. At your office, nothing happens until your one big thing and two supporting actions are complete. Everyone and everything else can wait. And if they cannot, which is almost never a reflection of true need, but rather an expectation you've trained into others, you process them quickly, without distraction, having made an intentional decision, then move back to your big thing and two supporters. You check e-mail, texts, and any other work-related communications only during a preset late-morning communications batch time, say 11 A.M., then again after lunch and once more at 4 P.M. People may call or text or e-mail or update or want to chat. You don't reply until you are ready.

You work at a deliberate pace and pause regularly to notice the day around you. You take in the sunshine pouring across your desk, the smell of coffee, and the little swirls of heat wafting into the air. You notice the state of your body, its position and how it feels. Throughout the day you'll change positions, walk, go outside, and constantly intersperse movement with work. You look around and see the partner who helped you start this company, your team whose members have been with you for years, and you're flooded with gratitude.

As the day unfolds, you quickly complete your one big thing and two supporting things, leaving everything else as bonus items that make you feel great. Problems arise, but you expect that and have cultivated a personal practice that allows you to stay calm and search for the solution from that intention of loving-kindness and mutual benefit. And though you'd rather not have had the problem, you find the possibility that would have stayed hidden had the problem never presented itself.

Wrapping up your day, you head home, phone again tucked away. You feel like you're ahead of the eight ball, aware of the moments that make up your day and proactively creating your life, rather than racing to respond on autopilot to other people's agendas, unaware of the vast amount of life's gifts that seem to race by before you can grasp them. You go out for a run, then ease into the evening with your family. You are not only physically but emotionally present. Checked in, on all levels. After dinner, you get a voice mail from the office with a true immediate need for response. You step away from your family, deal with it, then put your phone down, close your computer, and reengage. Before you doze off that night, you journal, revisiting the day, what went right, what went wrong, what you can learn from each, what you're grateful for, and what your big thing and two supporting things will be for tomorrow. You close your eyes. Life. Is. Good.

◎ ◎ ◎

So, which is closer to your life? Which scenario would you rather live, the reactive and unaware life or the intentional and aware? Your ability to live Scene Two is an outgrowth of three things:

- Awareness
- Intention
- Action

Awareness, waking up to what's in front of you, is the master key. By the time we reach adulthood, we're so distracted by the pull of speed, connectivity, expectations, and rules, we lose the ability to see and experience what's right in front of us. We become 99 percent unaware, and in doing so we lose the ability to choose and to act rather than react. By the way, those who tap into that 1 percent, who are awake and aware, not only tend to own their own lives but end up running the world.

Before you can make intelligent decisions, before you can stop reacting and start acting, you need to cultivate the ability to hit pause. To slow down just a bit, reconnect with who and what matters, to see what is really happening in the moment, to consider whose agenda you're responding to, then deliberately choose your actions based on that awareness and intention. So we need to begin cultivating your ability to turn off your autopilot.

The question is how. My awareness tool of choice is mindfulness, a word that it seems you can't get away from these days. It's the next big thing that's been around for thousands of years. Why the explosion in interest? Because the fallout of a global crush to live as mindlessly as possible has yielded astonishing levels of pain, and people are looking for a way out. In an odd irony, most of us spend our lives in the mindless pursuit of a state we've chosen to abandon and can return to at will. As Søren Kierkegaard lamented, "Most men pursue pleasure with such breathless haste that they hurry past it."

Mindfulness is about slowing down, noticing and seeing what is really happening in front of you in this moment, without the anxiety of expectation or the haze of regret. In this way, it is both a gateway to embracing the grace of each moment and the precursor to nearly every desired state, action, or experience that leads to a life well lived. Awareness is the seed of more aligned being and doing, which is why we explore it on Day 1.

It's also incredibly well researched. Turns out, beyond its impact on your ability to more readily see, choose, and create the life you want to live, a mindfulness practice can also improve memory, cognitive function, decision making, sleep, mood, and your ability to handle stress.

So how do you train the average Western mind, now boasting a shorter attention span than that of a goldfish, to focus and become more persistently aware?

Here are the basic instructions:

1. Find a comfortable place to sit where you won't
    be disturbed or distracted. Be sure to turn off all
    devices that might call you into "checking" mode.

If you use a timer app on a device (I recommend the Insight Timer), be sure to put the device into "Do not disturb" mode.

2. Sit with your spine erect but not rigid, and your head sitting gently in a neutral position.

3. Your eyes may be closed or slightly open.

4. Take a few long, slow breaths to settle in and bring your attention to your breathing.

5. Notice the sensation of your breath as it enters your body. Feel it entering your nostrils. Feel your chest and belly gently expand as you inhale and relax down as you exhale.

6. After a few breaths, notice where it is easier to hold your attention, the sensation of breath as it enters your nose or the sensation of your body expanding and relaxing as you breathe. Then focus your awareness on whichever sensation is an easier anchor.

7. Breathe gently and relax, holding your attention to the sensation of your breath.

8. At a certain point, maybe after just a few seconds, your mind will wander to thoughts or emotions. That's perfectly natural. Notice that, too. Then, with your next exhalation, silently say, "Thinking," and let that thought ride out with the breath as you refocus your attention on the breath. This may happen hundreds of times, especially in the beginning, and it's all fine.

9. Just keep coming back to your breath, without judgment or expectation.

For many people, it's much easier to begin this practice with someone else guiding them. In fact, that simple shift can turn it from something you "have" to do into something you "love" to do and look forward to. So I've created a 5-, 10-, 15-, and 20-minute guided audio mindfulness practice for you to download and listen to at GoodLifeProject.com/bookinsider.

All you need to do is download it to your chosen device and then, first thing in the morning, sit gently and listen. In fairly short order, you'll notice the effect. It will set up your day in a very different way. Over time, you'll find the calming and focusing effect will increase. You'll become more aware of the moment, less reactive, and more capable of pausing, seeing, intending, and choosing the actions that will put you back in charge of your life.

Daily Exploration:

Each day's exploration is designed to let you experience something that will fill one or more of your Good Life Buckets in a meaningful way. They are challenges that also provide specific ways to learn more about yourself and become more intentional about the way you live.

For today's exploration, I invite you to download to your phone or computer the guided mindfulness practices I've recorded for you. Remember, for the rest of this book, any time I offer you the opportunity to download or discover something online, unless I tell you otherwise, you'll find it at goodlifeproject.com/bookinsider.

Start with the five-minute version, first thing in the morning. All you need to do is follow the instructions. The practice is a great setup for a more aware and intentional day. Over time, you may find yourself wanting to organically move into the longer versions. You can make that shift if and when you're ready. It's also important to know that you're still doing fine if you never shift. If you choose to continue to listen each morning (can't recommend this enough) and grow into a longer practice, it'll begin to deliver more sustained benefits that will seep into nearly every area of your life.

At the end of the day, check in with your Good Life teammates to share your success and support one another. If inclined, share online, too. The more accountability you create, both privately and publicly, the more likely you'll be to stay with the practice long enough for it to become habit, and for you to feel the deepening effect of this beautiful practice.

Now, for those type A awareness challengers, here are a few more extras you might want to explore to reclaim awareness, intention, and choice:

1. **Go "push free" for 24 hours.** There's a good chance you have your computer, phone, watch, and any other wired device set to automatically "push" notifications to you every time someone else wants to take control of your life via e-mail, Facebook, Twitter, Instagram, Snapchat, and more. Here's your challenge: for a single day, turn off all automatic notifications on all devices. The more the thought of that gives you hives, the more reactive your life has become and the bigger the need to take it back. To become aware and choose.

2. **Set awareness triggers.** Set your watch, fitness tracker, smart watch, or smartphone to trigger a vibration alert mid-morning, just after lunch, mid-afternoon, and late afternoon. For phones, this can often be done by setting an alarm and choosing a vibration pattern instead of a sound. Whenever you feel the vibration alert, take a slow breath in and a slow breath out. You don't even have to stop what you're doing, but notice where your awareness is. Is your attention spinning into the future or trapped in the past? If so, take a few seconds to guide it gently back to the moment. Notice what's going on around you, what you're doing, who you're doing it with, and why. Notice whether your attention and your actions are placed on what truly matters most. If so, smile gently and take another slow breath. If not, guide it back to now, then do the same. The more you practice with these mini awareness interventions,

the more they become baked into the day and the easier it becomes to reclaim intention and take more deliberate action.

DAY 2

make EXERCISE more fun than SEX

When I first shared this idea, one comment made me giggle. "Dude, if exercise is more fun than sex, your sex life must suck." For most of us, the idea that exercise might be something that not only hones our bodies but also flips on our brains, arouses our senses, and connects us with others is just plain beyond belief. The notion that it might be something we crave rather than dread is downright absurd. No human, we think, actually *wants* to exercise. It's awful. It's hard, it hurts, it's humiliating, it's boring, it's isolating, and it's time out of the day that we just don't have. And the places to do it, ugh! Big, cold, scary, intimidating, unfriendly, ineffective, cliquey, and judgmental. This is what we've come to believe exercise is all about.

At the same time, the science is crystal clear. If we want to live good lives, we need to move our bodies. Nearly every marker of vitality—from reduced risk of heart disease, cancer, and diabetes to enhanced brain function, elevated mood, better ability to deal with stress, reduced anxiety and depression, and amped cognitive and physical abilities—is made better by exercise. Exercise is powerful medicine.

Problem is, most of us have come to believe exercise is something to be endured rather than embraced. That is tragic. Exercise done right adds to your life. Not just because of its many benefits, but because the very experience of it can be deeply enjoyable—when you do it right. Why the negative frame, then? Because much of the industry has been built around solutions that work for the industry, but not for the people it seeks to serve. Rows and rows of machines lock you into repetitive and astonishingly boring movement. Screens adorn every machine to distract you from how mind-numbing the experience is. To access your personal misery-distraction device, you need to put on headphones, further isolating you from the community and eliminating the possibility of conversation, friendship, and a sense of belonging. This all translates to dismal levels of long-term participation, terrible results beyond a small number of hardcore gym rats, and feelings of defeat, futility, self-loathing, boredom, and isolation.

It doesn't have to be this way. When we were kids, we ran around all day, climbed, danced, rolled, threw, caught, wiggled, jumped, cartwheeled, and kicked our way through the day. We worked hard, really hard, and loved it. The only reason we stopped is because we *had* to. Homework or dinner called us in. For those who played sports, there was the added experience of camaraderie, collaboration, shared effort, friendship, and belonging. We didn't call it exercise back then; we called it play, and we couldn't get enough. Our job today is to turn exercise back into play. To change repetition and boredom into novelty and engagement. To turn isolation and intimidation into friendship and belonging. To turn forced participation and futility into craved activity and transformative results.

Some in the industry have started to get it. They've realized the old way is broken and offered up activities, settings, and experiences that let us reclaim a sense of play, engagement, and community. SoulCycle turned indoor cycling into a near-addictive physical and cultural experience exploding across the country. CrossFit has become the fastest-growing phenomenon in the history of the fitness industry, reclaiming novelty, getting back to basics, cultivating a fierce commitment to community and progress. Its biggest challenge is likely not getting people to show up but stopping people from coming too often and pushing too hard.

There are, I'm sure, many other examples. You don't have to join a facility to bring joyful exercise back into your life. Get outside, if that's your style. Hike, ride, surf, trail run, Hula-Hoop. Join a group, team, or club. Take different classes. Whatever it is that makes you want to do more, find it, then do it. Look for things that demand not just physical effort but also mental focus and attention. When you engage your mind, time stops and effort becomes play. Even better, do it with others. Find a partner, group or community or rally a bunch of friends and create your own group or challenge to do together. This adds the element of friendship and accountability, especially in the early days when you're still getting fit enough to make it truly fun and desirable. Do this right and exercise becomes something you no longer fear and avoid. Much to your surprise, it becomes something you enjoy, then crave, even lust after and lament when you miss a day! You find yourself doing what, before, was unthinkable, reworking your day to include more of it, even sneaking out at lunch for an "exercise quickie!"

Don't stop there. Exercise is great. But truth is, it's not enough.

You may have seen all the headlines about sitting over the past few years. Sitting is the new smoking. It is now listed as a major risk factor for a wide variety of diseases. Even worse, *exercising for 30 to 60 minutes does not come close to making up for the damage done by sitting.* Actually, it's not really sitting that is taking us down. It's the act of remaining static and inactive for long periods of time in any position. We are built for motion. Nearly every beneficial mind and body system is optimized when we move and slowly shuts down when we don't. The only way to counter this is to bring movement back into our days. Not in one intense burst, but woven throughout. We can do this any number of ways.

Set a vibration alarm to go off on your watch or phone every 50 minutes, then get up and walk around or move for 10. Grab a headset and turn every phone call into a walking or stretching call. Turn all meetings into standing meetings. This will have the added benefit of forcing people to get to the point faster. My friend Emiliya Zhivotovskaya, founder of The Flourishing Center and the Certificate in Applied Positive Psychology, switched to a standing desk. That wasn't enough. She bought a cheap mini treadmill, took off the side rails, and walks on it while working. She takes every call on a headset while moving and regularly takes mini breaks to stretch and to do light calisthenics, yoga, and dare I say, even a bit of pole dancing! Point is, it's not that hard to bring gentle movement back into your day if you choose to make it a priority.

Exercise and movement. There are perhaps no better therapies for nearly everything that ails us. These two elixirs are powerful Vitality Bucket fillers. Done with intention, they can also be joyful, life-affirming, connection-driven parts of life that prime many of the same neurological and chemical responses unleashed by, you guessed it, sex.

Before we wrap this conversation, we should probably address the elephant in the bedroom. Can you really make exercise more fun than sex? C'mon, I know you've been wondering. Even more intriguing, could sex actually count as exercise? A 2013 study published in the journal *PLOS One* looked at the question. Strapping armbands on 21 couples that averaged 22 years old, researchers measured energy expenditure during sex and running (not at the same time). On average, participants burned about 85 calories, or 3.6 calories per minute, during moderate-intensity sex. The same participants burned about 244 calories over 30 minutes of running. What does that tell us? It certainly counts as vigorous movement, and maybe even moderate exercise. With care and the right intention, both sex and exercise can be a lot of fun, involve other people, and have mood and health-elevating effects. But, it's probably a good idea to bring them into your life as separate good life interventions.

Daily Exploration:

Step 1—Add movement.

Think about your average day. If no day is average, think about today. What can you do to bring more gentle movement into it? Can you walk at an easy pace while doing anything? Can you take breaks every hour to get up and move and stretch a little? You don't have to exert yourself much or sweat; you just have to move. For today, at a bare minimum, challenge yourself to move at least 10 minutes out of every hour. Set a vibration alarm to remind yourself, in case you get lost in some activity. Decide what you'll do in advance so you don't have to waste time choosing.

Step 2—Add exercise.

If you loathe the thought of going to the gym, then don't. There are now many options to explore. Search your area to see if you can find a place that offers activities that (a) sound like they could be fun; (b) engage your mind, along with your body; (c) involve a fair amount of novelty and change, not just sustained repetition; and (d) integrate a sense of community. Look online, ask friends, read the local paper, whatever you need to do to start the process of discovery. It may take a little time to find the activity and community that makes you want to come back. That's okay. If you can't find anything local, then check out some of the growing online offerings, with wonderful streaming class options. I have included a bunch of resources and links at goodlifeproject. com/bookinsider to get you started. Choose one, put your first "trial run" on your calendar, and make it happen. Then journal about the experience.

DAY 3

SNOOZE to LIVE

Sleep. Ugh. Do we really have to go there? Short answer: yes. It is one of the most effective Vitality Bucket fillers (and also killers). Plus, it's one of the things that flow most powerfully into both your Contribution and Connection Buckets. When we sleep, everything gets better. Our health, energy, strength, ability to think and create, mood, resilience, ability to handle adversity, cultivate relationships, do great work, and radiate light and calm all dramatically increase. When we don't sleep, every one of these decreases.

Sleep disruption is a massive problem. According to the National Sleep Foundation:

- 40 million people in the United States alone have a chronic sleep disorder.

- 62 percent of U.S. adults have trouble sleeping at least a few nights a week.

- 30 percent of the general population experience insomnia at some point over the course of a year.

Thing is, poor sleep doesn't just make us cranky and tired; it also wreaks havoc on nearly every system in the body. When we're sleep deprived, our risk of chronic diseases like hypertension, diabetes, depression, obesity, and cancer skyrocket. Sleep loss is associated with a 200 percent rise in cancer and a 100 percent rise in heart disease. It also decreases our memory and ability to think. A recent study revealed sleeping less than six hours a day for two weeks has an effect on your brain similar to blowing a 0.10 on an alcohol test, which would make you too drunk to drive. We see this impairment across all ages.

Dr. Avi Sadeh of Tel Aviv University studied the effects of a slightly shortened sleep period in fourth and sixth graders. After three days of getting just 30 minutes less sleep, the average sixth grader's abilities plummeted to that of a fourth grader.[3] A second study from the University of Minnesota revealed that the average A student slept 36 minutes more than the average D student.[4] Moved by this and other evidence, a high school in Edina, Minnesota, pushed its start time from 7:25 A.M. to 8:30 A.M. and saw a stunning jump in SAT scores from the top 10 percent of students, from 1288 to 1500.

It's not just our brains and overall health that take a hit. When we don't sleep enough, we get fatter. Sleep disruption drops our metabolism and ramps up food cravings, likely due to their effect on the hormones ghrelin and leptin. Ghrelin tells us to eat, and leptin tells us to stop. When we're sleep deprived, we're all ghrelin and not enough leptin. Translation: we'll eat pretty much anything that's not glued down, including the stuff in the far corner of the top shelf that we can only reach from the stepladder! Add that to a metabolism that slows when you're sleep deprived and dysregulation of fat cells and insulin, and you end up with the perfect fat-heaping, inflammation-loading, vitality-killing storm.

Many people look to medication to "treat" their sleep disturbances because it seems like the quick and easy way to fix the problem. While that may be the appropriate path for some, medication comes with potential risks that include drowsiness, amnesia, headache, mental impairment, uncontrollable shaking, weakness, cancer, falling, tinnitus, increased risk of dementia, addiction, and death. Many medications also actually put you into more of a hypnotic state than a true deep sleep. That may leave you feeling like you've been out cold, but there is increasing doubt about whether it really provides anywhere near the restorative benefit true sleep delivers.

Which brings us to an interesting question. Actually, two.

First, how much sleep do we really need?

The National Institutes of Health suggest that school-age children need at least ten hours of sleep daily, teens need nine to ten hours, and adults need seven to eight hours.[5] Research shows us that people who sleep either less than five hours or more than nine hours a night fare worse than those who average seven to eight hours. Are some people outliers? Of course. Are you one? Maybe. But do you really want to take that chance? If you assume you are an exception to the rule but you're wrong, the price you pay could be catastrophic over time. Better to start with the assumption that, with regard to sleep needs, you are typical. Then do everything needed to optimize your sleep before accepting that you may be an outlier. I have friends who slept five to six hours a night for years and just assumed that was all they needed. After optimizing their sleep and bumping it up to seven to eight hours, though, they realized how wrong they were. That brings us to the second question.

What's the best way to get it? There are four steps:

- Rule out/take care of sleep apnea
- Build your sleep hygiene
- Track and hack
- Train your brain

Today's daily exploration is all about these four steps. We're going to walk through exactly what to do to optimize your sleep and, hopefully, minimize your need for medication.

Daily Exploration:

First, find out if the reason you're sleeping poorly is because you have something called sleep apnea. It's when we stop breathing while we sleep, and about 5 percent of us have it. If you really want a definitive answer, you can be tested in a sleep lab or use a home detection device. You can also get a good sense for whether you might have the most common form, obstructive sleep apnea (OSA) by completing the Berlin questionnaire for OSA.[6] The questionnaire isn't definitive, though, so if you have any doubts, see a health care professional specializing in sleep. I've included links to sleep lab resources and also a downloadable version of the Berlin assessment at goodlifeproject.com/bookinsider.

If you do have OSA or either of the less common forms of apnea, don't rely only on the ideas that follow. Work with a professional. You may also discover that you have apnea only when sleeping on your back, so a simple change in position may go a long way toward helping. Once you've ruled out or accommodated for apnea, focus on the sleep hygiene basics.

1. **Keep a consistent sleeping and waking time, even on the weekends.** Your body has an internal clock. When you constantly change sleep and wake times, the clock gets screwy and has trouble signaling your body and brain to start the process of winding down. Research also shows the best window for sleep time is between about 10 and 11 P.M. After that, many people start to cycle into a more alert state, making it harder to fall asleep for a few hours. To the extent your life lets you find a consistent sleep time and you can fit it in between 10 and 11 P.M., do it.

2. **Build a sleep ritual.** Do the same things at the same times every evening. Rituals can be calming and help draw you away from the stress or high-alert state of your day. They signal to your body and brain that it's time to prepare for sleep. Your mind and body also need time to wind down before bed, so build

relaxing activities into your routine. For example, write in a journal for 10 minutes, read a book for 10 to 20 minutes, listen to calming music, do breathing exercises, or meditate. As much as possible, try to make it the exact same action at the same time every day.

3. **Don't nap after noon.** Napping can be a great way to refresh. But if you have trouble sleeping at night, it is possible that an afternoon nap may disrupt your ability to fall asleep and stay asleep at night. And truthfully, if you're so wiped out that you need a nap before noon, that's another potential sign of substantial sleep deprivation.

4. **Exercise.** A fairly intense level of exercise seems to have the greatest impact on sleep, rather than low-level activity, but even light exercise is better than none. Some research shows the best time is about two to four hours before sleep. The mechanism may be the body's need to recover and repair as well as the sleep signal that is triggered when your body temperature falls slowly, as it does in the hours that follow exercise. For the same reason, it's likely not a good idea to exercise right before trying to go to sleep, with the exception, of course, of sex, which releases a veritable cocktail of calming chemistry into your bloodstream afterward.

5. **Turn your room into a sleep den.** Your bedroom should be cool, between 60 and 67 degrees, as quiet as possible, and free from light. If that's just impossible (hey, I live in NYC; I get it), consider using blackout curtains, eyeshades, earplugs, a white noise machine, humidifier, fan, or other device. And remember, your sleep den is for sleep, sex,

and reading. No other activities. No TV or other screen time.

6. **Sleep on a comfortable mattress and pillows.** Make sure your mattress is comfortable and supportive. Between your mattress and pillows, you want to get as close as possible to a neutral spine, regardless of whether you sleep on your back or side.

7. **Avoid bright light in the evening, especially from screens.** One of the triggers for sleep is the release of melatonin in your body. Unfortunately, exposure to bright light, especially the blue frequencies emitted by computers, TVs, and handheld devices, can dramatically suppress melatonin levels and end up making it far harder to fall sleep. Turn down the lights a few hours before bed, and stay away from screens. If you must be on a screen, use a blue-light limiter app like f.lux, which automatically drops the blue light as the sun sets. You can download it at justgetflux.com.

8. **Avoid alcohol, cigarettes, caffeine, and heavy meals in the evening.** Alcohol, cigarettes, and caffeine can disrupt sleep. Eating big or spicy meals can cause discomfort from indigestion that can make it hard to sleep. Finish eating at least two to three hours before bedtime, and if you are sensitive to caffeine, stop consuming it after noon.

9. **If you can't sleep, don't just lie there.** Get out of bed, go to a different room, and do something relaxing until you feel tired. It is best to take work materials, computers, and televisions out of the sleeping environment. Use your bed only for sleep, light reading as part of a sleep ritual (non-digital),

and sex to strengthen the association between bed and sleep.

10. **Don't freak out if you wake in the middle of the night.** If you tend to wake up after about three or four hours of sleep, that's not necessarily a bad thing. In fact, research shows that the eight-hours-in-one-shot approach to sleep may be somewhat of a modern invention. When people are removed from all artificial sleep cues, one study found, they start to shift to a sleep pattern of about four hours asleep, 30 to 60 minutes awake, then another three to four hours asleep.[7] Reports of sleep throughout history often reference a "first sleep" and a "second sleep." And many highly accomplished creators have written about how they would work during the time between the first and second sleeps and how it was their most powerful window for being creative. What stops us from falling back to sleep isn't that we can't sleep. It's the anxiety story we make up that says, "This is wrong, I'm supposed to sleep eight straight hours, I'll never sleep again." Instead of freaking out and telling yourself there's something wrong, just know it's actually very natural to sleep, wake for a bit, then sleep again. Do some breathing or meditating, listen to gentle music, and you will very likely find yourself drifting back off into your natural second sleep.

Beyond these sleep hygiene basics, you may want to explore a fairly new approach to sleep training that is gaining converts and proving to be very effective, even for people who have had trouble sleeping for years. It's called mindfulness-based therapy for insomnia (MBT-I). It combines many of the best practices of cognitive therapy for insomnia and mindfulness-based stress reduction. I share some resources and links at goodlifeproject.com/bookinsider.

Funny enough, when I was in the throes of dealing with insomnia caused by tinnitus, I developed my own approach to reclaiming my sleep that closely tracks MBT-I. I still struggle with sleep at times, but now it's tied to periods of high stress (self-imposed; I've really gotta stop that) rather than the piercing anxiety and fear that addled me as I learned to be okay with the sound in my head.

It's also a great idea to keep a sleep journal. Write down what time you went to bed, what the conditions were in the room (light, sound, temperature, humidity), what your ritual was, what was on your mind before going to sleep, how you think you slept, how often you awakened, what time you rose, whether you rose naturally or with an alarm (or multiple alarms and snoozes), and how you felt upon rising. For even more precision, you sleep hackers might want to explore some of the cool technology and apps that automatically track these things, along with breathing and time in the different levels of sleep. I use a number of these myself. Two faves include the Fitbit wrist activity tracker and the Beddit sleep tracker.

You don't have to do this for life, but doing a bit of journaling and tracking in the beginning can really help you better understand the factors that make the biggest difference in your ability to become a sleep savant.

One last thought: If you've been on medication for any period of time and your goal is to transition off it, please talk to your health care provider about the best way to do that. Cold turkey may not be good, as many medications create some blend of physical and psychological dependency.

DAY 4

TAKE A GREEN DAY

As a young mom with a typically fraught schedule, my friend Jadah Sellner was burned out, stressed out, and unhealthy. Looking to reclaim her vitality in 2011, she decided to try an experiment. She knew she wanted to become healthier and to feel better, both for herself and for her family. Sellner wanted to have tons of energy to play with her daughter and be there for her husband. But she didn't have the time, motivation, or willpower to make big changes to the way she fueled her body. Instead, she decided to commit to a single change in behavior. One simple thing—how hard could that be?

Every day, she would drink a simple green smoothie. Perfect solution for a mom on the go, all her fruits and veggies in one quick, portable package. No need to worry about cooking multiple meals and tons of cleanup afterward. One of the first challenges, of course, was the basic assumption about what a green smoothie has to taste like. As a general rule, when the uninitiated envision a big glass of green stuff, the word *yummy* doesn't come to mind. She knew she'd have to find the right mixtures of fruits and veggies, not only to make them go down easy, but to turn green smoothies into a daily treat. So she set to work. Sellner loved researching and coming up with new smoothie recipes. It was like playtime, with a healthy benefit. Delightful blended mixes came together, and Sellner started her daily dose of deliciousness.

Within a matter of months, that single act began to transform her health, giving Jadah boundless energy and spurring the loss of 25 pounds without her even trying. Inspired to share her discovery, Sellner eventually teamed with her friend Jen Hansard to turn her smoothie habit into Contribution and Connection Bucket–filling engines with the launch of the global Simple Green Smoothies movement.

For now, let's focus on what really happened with her smoothie-a-day habit, why it became such a powerful Vitality Bucket filler for her, and how it can do the same for you. We'll start with why a simple smoothie can sometimes be so much more effective than a radical change in diet.

Stanford University professor B. J. Fogg has spent years researching how we create habits.[8] Especially ones that help make us healthy. He found that one of the keys is to chunk the desired behavior down to its smallest possible element. An element so "doable" that it'd be near-impossible not to do it. Why? Because the secret to long-term success in any endeavor is not magic but sustained action over time. And we don't do anything for long unless (1) it is easy to start and (2) we can keep doing it long enough for it to become a habit. The more we repeat something, the more automatic it becomes. And, here's the thing: once we've built that basic behavior into our lives and it has become a habit, the duration and intensity often expand on their own.

For Jadah, starting with a simple green smoothie a day was far more effective than starting with a head-to-toe overhaul in diet because the latter would have required so much change, willpower, and motivation she never would have sustained it. This also happens to be a pretty big part of the reason so many large, disruptive personal quests for fitness and weight loss fail so miserably. With rare exception, one simple shift outperforms 100 huge changes, because the one thing is far more likely to be sustained than the 100 things that will inevitably melt down in days.

There is one other big reason to approach better nutrition or even movement and exercise in this way. As they turn into habits, certain types of behaviors can become what *The Power of Habit* author Charles Duhigg calls "keystone" habits. These seemingly small changes create a cascade effect. They trigger a series of follow-on changes that never would have happened had you tried to do them all at once. You start with a simple green smoothie a day. You wake up every morning and, without even thinking about it, blend up a yummy beverage based on plants and fruits. Because it's so easy, you keep doing it, and over a few weeks or months it becomes an automatic behavior.

The veggies and fruits begin to work their magic on your body and mind, giving you more energy, lowering inflammation, and helping you shed pounds from your frame. Not only do you start to feel better, but you feel better about yourself and your ability to create change. These feelings plant a new seed: What might happen if I started walking for 10 minutes a day? The cascade of simple new behaviors begins, each unlocking another until you find yourself transformed. Not through fierce conviction or superhuman will, but through simple, daily, Vitality Bucket–filling action.

Now it's your turn.

Daily Exploration:

For today's exploration, we're going to take a page from Jadah Sellner's playbook. While it would be wonderful to eventually make the shift to lots of whole foods and plants, what we really care about is your first step. What better way to begin than to follow in Sellner's footsteps? Your action for today is to blend up one simple green smoothie. To make it easier, I've asked Jadah, along with good friends Crazy Sexy Life founder and vital lifestyle crusader Kris Carr and *The Plantpower Way* authors Julie Piatt and

Rich Roll, to each share two of their yummiest recipes. You can find them over at GoodLifeProject.com/bookinsider.

Of course, if you find yourself digging the green smoothie and want to keep going, you're welcome to try out all six recipes, one a day. If you'd love even more variety to keep building this delicious new good life habit, check out their full-length recipe books, too. And, just as we do every day, by the end of today, be sure to share your smoothie adventure with your Good Life teammates and post about your smoothie exploits to inspire and find support in our online community.

DAY 5

get your GRATITUDE on

Tell me if this has ever happened to you.

You work really hard on something. Maybe it's a project or an idea. A beautiful offering, event, or gathering. It's something you've created and put your heart and soul into. It's all done. Then you stand back to take it in. If it involves others, you invite them in or give it to them. Then it hits you. For the first time, you notice. The glaring typo. The aberrant brushstroke. The missed stitch. The burned dish. The off comment. The weird glitch that leads to an unkind review or remark. You wish you could unsee or undo it. But you can't. And now, even though everything is amazing, you can't stop thinking about the one bad thing. People thank you, compliment you, offer gratitude for what you've done. Still, you don't hear it; your brain is trapped in a sea of negativity.

As someone who is constantly creating things and putting them into the world, I come face-to-face with this all day, every day. One-star book reviews, misunderstood comments, people who just don't get me, those with completely different styles or tastes, desires or interests. Then there are the times when I've just plain screwed up. These moments and experiences aren't fun. For a long time, they would weigh heavily on me. But that wasn't the worst part. The worst part was that they would so consume me, I would have trouble seeing and taking in the 99 percent that was amazing. Turns out I'm not alone.

Through an ironic quirk of evolution, our brains have developed in a way that, on the one hand, keeps us alive, but on the other, makes us just a tad downbeat and neurotic. Not all of us, but many of us. We are wired to focus on the sucky side of life. Scientists call it the negativity bias. We latch onto the stuff that goes wrong and refuse to let go, sometimes for years. Meanwhile, the stuff that goes right we barely acknowledge. This can lead to a pretty warped situation. From the outside looking in, we're living awesome lives and everything seems to be going right. But from the inside looking out, all we see are the stumbles or negative experiences. The drag can become obsessive and even, poorly handled, pull us toward not just pessimism and compulsion but anxiety and depression. So what can we do? How do we battle this wiring?

One way is to proactively bring so many more positive experiences into each day that it becomes harder and harder to ignore how good things really are. That can help tip the mindset from down and out to upbeat and optimistic. For many, though, it's still not enough. That nasty little negativity bias, compounded by the everyday challenges life throws our way, keeps us from seeing the good, no matter how much there is.

Professor Martin Seligman, known as the father of positive psychology, wondered whether there was a way to rewire our brains for positivity and pull them out of the downward spiral. Turns out there is. Actually, there are many ways, but as Seligman discovered, one of the most powerful mood elevators is so simple, it's easy to write off as fluff. Just some pop psychology quackery. Except it's not.

So what's the key? Gratitude. Seligman realized that often negativity came from an inability to see and be grateful for what was right in life. He wondered what might happen if specific exercises forced you to acknowledge the awesome side of life and then express your gratitude for it. Would that counter the pull of negativity? Turns out it would. And it does.

Over the past 10 years, gratitude has been hailed as one of the most universally effective mindset boosters and happiness enhancers on the planet. It's also been heavily researched and validated beyond the realm of anecdotal self-help. But that still leaves us with a question. How do we build gratitude? How do we break out of the doom-and-gloom cocoon and see more of what's right in life?

One of the most popular gratitude-building exercises is the gratitude journal. The idea is to regularly write down what you're grateful for. There are many variations. In his book *Flourish: A Visionary New Understanding of Happiness and Well-being*,[9] Seligman offers his own research-backed approach, which he calls the Three Blessings. I'll describe the process in detail below. It will be the first option in today's exploration. The blessings are actually fun to do, and they don't take much time.

A quick note on how often to do them. Seligman suggests a daily approach. Sonja Lyubomirsky, another leading voice in positive psychology believes that instead of doing them daily, you should test what feels right for you. In her book *The How of Happiness: A New Approach to Getting the Life You Want*,[10] she suggests that a daily practice may start to feel forced and repetitive and cause the exercise to lose its power. In Lyubomirsky's research, once a week seemed to be the sweet spot for most people. So play with it. If it starts to feel like a rote or repetitive exercise and doesn't seem to be doing anything to lift your mood or change your view of life, spread it out a bit.

The second gratitude builder is talked about far less often but has been shown in Seligman's research to pretty much crush almost every other happiness-boosting exercise. Seligman calls it the gratitude visit, and it's the second option in today's bucket-filling exploration.

Hang onto your hats; it's time to get your gratitude on!

Daily Exploration:

Option 1—The Three Blessings

In *Flourish,* Seligman offers specific instructions to be followed every night for at least a week (and as long after as you like):

- Write down three things that went well today. They can be big things ("I proposed to the love of my life and she said yes"), or simple everyday things (my daughter told me she loved me and gave me a hug and kiss before leaving for school).

- For each of the three things, answer the question "Why did this happen?"

Make tonight your first night. Keep track of how your lens on life and general mood change over time. And, as Lyubomirsky suggests, experiment a bit to find the perfect frequency for you. Start out daily for a week. If that feels good and it's moving your mindset needle, keep it up. If not, explore once a week, twice a month, or whatever feels right for you.

Option 2—The Gratitude Visit

The gratitude visit will take a bit more work, but it will also be worth the effort. Seligman's research showed that a single experience can create changes in mindset that are still there a month later. Look back on your life and think of someone who made a difference to you. It could have been someone who helped you out when you were in need, someone who encouraged you or taught you something or any other person who did something that made your life better. Two other qualifiers: it should be someone you never thanked, and someone who is close enough for you to visit in person.

Next, write a letter to that person describing, in specifics, what they did for you and how it affected you. Share what you're up to now and let them know how often you revisit their kindness. It should be a full page, or about 300 words.

Now here's where it gets fun, and also where it might challenge you a bit. Do it anyway. Call the person up and tell them you'd love to stop by to say a quick hello. Don't tell them exactly why you're coming. You want to keep it a surprise, if you can. Then go visit your person and read your letter to them, face-to-face.

When you return home, spend a few minutes journaling about how the experience went and how it made you feel. Then, if you're inspired, share a bit about the experience in our online group.

DAY 6

DANCE like NOBODY'S WATCHING
(BECAUSE they're NOT)

Something kind of magical happened when I sat down to record a conversation with Elizabeth Gilbert, author of *Eat, Pray, Love* and *Big Magic*. It was like the whole exchange happened in some sort of suspended space. The room filled with a certain lightness. Wisdom rained down like drops from heaven, but without all the heaviness that often comes with being schooled by someone you sense is profoundly in the know.

When Gilbert's episode aired, the response validated everything I had felt in the room. People e-mailed and posted and shared. They couldn't stop talking about it, offering how they kept listening over and over, taking notes, laughing, crying, and loving every moment. It just made them happy. Apparently, this response to her presence is not all that unusual. What was it about her, I wondered, that made her so magical? Sure, there is the fact that she openly believes in magical thinking; we all want to find a little more fairy dust in our lives. There was the seemingly endless flow of stories and wisdom and hope that tumble ever so effortlessly from her. But there was something else. Something I didn't key in on until I the saw the transcript of our conversation.

Reading through the text, a single word surrounded by brackets kept appearing over and over. There was not a single minute that passed without the transcriber noting that she "[laughs]." Was it just that I was so funny? Anyone who knows me knows the answer to that question is a definite no. It was all coming from her. She was cracking herself up. Gilbert was astonishingly comfortable in her own skin, unapologetically herself, unconditionally joyful. She made me want to be the same, and she gave me hope that I could let go and lighten up, just like her.

I jumped on Instagram shortly afterward to check her feed. There I found a parade of pictures and images that radiated not just joy but, again, comfort. One shot showed her made up for the camera and stage. The next showed her without a stitch of makeup, her hair up, glasses on, with a touch of bed-head and the comment "If you're wondering what an author looks like when she wakes up on the long-awaited morning of her book launch: here you go! The glamour never ends." Also in her stream was a video of her dancing around in old sweats like nobody was watching, while two friends played drums and bass behind her. She was telling the world, "I'm real, and I'm not going to hide from you. Let's dance!"

Brené Brown, same thing. She's spent decades researching shame and has shared openly about her own struggles with it in all parts of her life. At the same time, she is unapologetically, shamelessly herself. She makes no excuses and brings all of her funny, sardonic, brilliant, offbeat, nonconformist, playful Texan self to everything she does. As with Gilbert, there is this sense of confident ease, true lightness and joy that radiates from her. And I wondered, why don't we all act this way?

That's when it dawned on me. You can't just choose to be joyful.

For some, there may be deep wounds, layers of trauma or pathology that neither this nor any book is capable of healing. If that is you, by the way, please take the steps needed to find someone truly qualified to help you reconnect with your beautiful and worthy self.

For far more people, though, there's something else going on. Something that stifles their ability to just choose joy.

Before you can choose joy, you have to choose *you*.

That's what Gilbert and Brown have done. There is a certain heaviness that seeps into every part of life when you walk through each day trying to be someone else. The energy put into hiding who you are and then building any number of alter egos to satisfy society's expectations of who you are eventually becomes crushing. You may be able to keep up the illusion of survival or even joy for a short time, but in the end it always drags you down. The longer you wear the mask, the harder it is to keep up the facade, to muster a modicum of civility, let alone joy. At some point, you have to choose. Will you continue to hide, living under the weight of expectation, or allow yourself to be seen?

The moment you choose you, the heaviness begins to ease. Seeds of lightness begin to grow. That doesn't mean all of life's problems drop away, but you get to turn loose the wellspring of energy that was being used to prop up the illusion, using it instead on the process of reconnecting with people, joy, meaning, and lightness.

So why don't we all just stop hiding, then? Why don't we roll through each day unapologetically ourselves? What stops us from dancing like nobody's watching?

Fear. We're terrified. Afraid of being judged for our weird, goofball, bizarre, quirky selves. Sadly, it often takes being stripped bare before we're willing to step into that place where we just don't care what others think or say. Many of the people I've known in life who've found that place of full expression and unapologetic joy have also been through substantial trials. They've hit the proverbial, and sometimes literal, rock bottom. When you land in that place and are forced to examine who and what truly matter, you realize life is short. There is a cost to living in the shadows. You've been judged as fiercely as you could be judged; you have nothing left to lose by just being you. That's when the renewal begins. That's when the light shines through.

Does that mean you need to manufacture or invite into your existence a full-life face-plant before you can step into the essence of who you are? Of course not. It just means you have to begin to choose you. Take baby steps. First in private. Then, if you feel emboldened, bring that gorgeous self, the one that's been yearning to get out, to a friend. Then a few more, and a few more. Then, who knows, maybe to the world.

Acclaimed creative coach Cynthia Morris decided to go public with both her artistic and her goofball self at around the same time. Actually the goofball part came much more easily for her. She would post videos of herself dancing on YouTube, just like Elizabeth Gilbert did on Instagram. Did some people think she was nuts? Sure. But who really cared? Tons more thought she was awesome and wanted more. The bigger move, for her, was stepping publicly into her artistic side. She challenged herself to post her work online on a regular basis. Every week it became a little easier until, watercolor by watercolor, she freed herself to be the artist she'd kept trapped inside for years. People loved her and her work. She chose herself, and from that emerged a deeper level of joy.

Married father of three Kristoffer Carter had a senior leadership position at a fast-growing tech company in Chicago. He was respected and appreciated for his work and the effect he had on cultivating the company's award-winning culture. He was a responsible adult, a family man. At the same time, he spent half of last year's Camp GLP running around dressed in a unicorn costume and holding a megaphone, and he regularly posts videos of himself on the Internet dancing as any number of cartoon characters. That same playful, offbeat self shows up in all parts of his life. Might some people think it was off-putting? Maybe. But, as Dr. Seuss offered, "Those who mind don't matter, and those who matter don't mind." They're not his people. Enough of those who matter love him in all his quirky glory, beloved and in demand in all parts of business and life. His willingness to choose himself, to drop the mask, unlocked his ability to choose joy. When truth meets joy, radiance ensues.

Amanda Palmer, an artist and author of *The Art of Asking*, reflecting on the loss of her dear friend Anthony, summed it up beautifully in a talk in Boston:

> It's stupid to be safe. Because ultimately, usually whatever that is, wherever you don't want to go, whatever that risk is, whatever the unsafe place is, that really is the gift that you have to give. . . . And whatever you think is just going to be pleasing, and whatever you think will make people like you, that's not your gift. Your gift is that spot over there that no one else can see, and you're like, 'Oh, do I really want to share that? Do I really want to say it? Do I really want to try it?' And you do.

So, what about you? Will people think you're nuts if you go public with your goofy, quirky, artistic, nerdy self? Sure, some will. Most won't. Those who matter will fall madly in love with you and want to be in your orbit. And, the biggest revelation of all, very few people are even watching in the first place. Nobody really cares but you. So why not take the first step to being unapologetically joyful? Start by being unapologetically you.

Daily Exploration:

I've got two explorations for you today, depending how bold you feel like being.

Option 1—Take baby steps
Think about a part of you that is longing to see the light of day. Take out your journal and, in a full page, describe that person. Who would you be if you knew with 100-percent certainty that nobody was watching and you would not be judged? Go ahead and write. I'll wait.
Back? Good. Now ask yourself, "What tiny thing can I do to bring a little piece of that person to the surface?" Maybe you can share that snippet with a trusted friend or group, or a loving partner, or online if that's where you're most comfy. Decide

what action you will take, then do it before this day ends. Then come back to your journal and share a quick reflection on what happened. And if you're inclined, do it again tomorrow. Then the next day, and the next.

Option 2—The Nuclear "Dance Like Nobody's Watching (Because They're Not)"

We're going to get physical and have a little fun. Maybe dancing around is your thing, maybe it's not. But I have not yet met the human who has zero connection to music or rhythm. You may want to glide across the floor to Sinatra, shake it down to Madonna, or groove to Aretha. In any case, choose music that makes you want to move, even if it's just tapping your foot while biting your lower lip and bopping your head. Close the doors, close the windows, turn down the lights if you want, turn up the music (or put on your headphones). Steer clear of anything you might bang into. For a single song, let your body groove a bit.

I'm horrified to admit, back when I was in law school, my private jam was George Michael's "Freedom! '90." Went nuts to it before every final. Alone. In my room. It was not pretty, but it felt awesome. Find your groove and do it every day. Then, if and when you're ready, invite others to join in. Maybe it's the kids or your partner or friends. Maybe it's a buddy on Skype. Doesn't really matter, just make it a regular thing. Once you feel more comfy with your bad, goofy self, what might happen if you shared a little dance party with your friends by posting a video online? Start out by posting in our Good Life Project private group, if you like. We may even have a bit of a weekly video dance party there.

Why focus on this one thing? Because our bodies and minds unwind together. Through a lot of years teaching all different forms of movement, from yoga to kickboxing to indoor cycling and more, I've realized that you don't always have to start with the mind. In fact, it's often more effective to start with your body. Moving in ways that push your comfort and free you up to be more playful, to move the way you want to, not the way you think you're supposed to, starts to trickle back up to your brain. Those maniacally locked-down pathways start to unwind and open up.

Releasing physical holding patterns can unconsciously begin to unlock psychological holding patterns. It starts by getting real for five minutes alone in the dark, but soon enough, you may find yourself emboldened to bring more of yourself to each day in a thousand small ways. Each a small crack in the mask, until eventually it starts to fall away.

Try it on for size. What's the worst that could happen? You feel a little weird, have a little fun, get a little sweaty, and maybe, just maybe, rediscover and reveal those parts of yourself that have been stuck inside for far too long.

DAY 7

OWN the UNKNOWN

I remember it like it was yesterday. The tail end of sixth grade, in the way back of the basement at Ellie's house. We'd just returned from my first-ever double date—or, for that matter, anything resembling any kind of date. Didi Conn, soon to be immortalized as Frenchy in the screen version of *Grease*, played the lead as Debby Boone crooned *You Light Up My Life* over the crackling sound system. Beyond the song and Didi, I don't remember a thing. Not because I was eleven, but because the entire time, I was shaking with terror and largely incapable of hearing anything but the sound of my heart pounding through my chest.

I was consumed by a question. Did she or didn't she? I mean, we'd hung out at JoJo's Pizza after school for weeks. But this was a whole different thing. Was it a *Date* date, or just a date? Did she capital *L Like* me, or just like me?

Now, back in the far reaches of her basement, I was about to find out. Would we kiss? Would this become the single greatest moment of my life? Maybe of all human history? Or would we just sit uncomfortably in the dark, stammering and giggling, the air riddled with prepubescent anxiety before I'd chicken out and leave? Please God, send me a signal! I just needed to know. Does she or doesn't she?

Fast-forward 25 years. The year was 2001, the day before 9/11. With a wife and three-month-old daughter, and without knowing the pain that would soon blanket my city, I signed a six-year lease for a floor in a building in Hell's Kitchen, NYC. My quest was to launch and build a yoga center that would become an oasis. I had no idea of the abyss I was stepping into. Months in, burned-out, massively sleep-deprived, and having largely abandoned the very practice I was teaching to keep others sane, I sat on the living room couch, head in hands. Everything had been turned upside down. My dream. My business. My plans. My confidence. My sanity. My life. And I had a family looking to me to make everything okay. I wanted the uncertainty that seemed to define every breath, every thought, every moment of my waking life to stop. I just wanted it to be a year from then. Then I'd know whether it all works out. Or not. If I failed, I failed. So be it. I could live with that and move on.

There's this odd irony in life. I wish it weren't so. Every breakthrough is preceded by great uncertainty. If you think about it, this makes sense. The only way to avoid uncertainty, to come close to guaranteed success in an endeavor, is if you've done it before, or someone else has. At that point, why bother? You're no longer creating, you're replicating, checking off yet another largely inevitable outcome. It may be easier. It may carry less angst. But it will also matter far less to you and to those you seek to serve.

Life's greatest moments live in the space between desire and attainment. It's not the getting that makes life good, it's the seeking, even when that seeking demands not just action but surrender. The moment your object of desire becomes a foregone conclusion, the quest loses its potential to change you. Your life becomes a series of reruns, and that gets old fast.

Uncertainty may bring unease, but it also brings a vital energy, the exhilaration of creation. Without uncertainty, there is no possibility. We end up living not in "the arena," as Teddy Roosevelt describes, but in "the gray twilight that knows neither victory nor defeat."

There is no perfect moment. No time when you will know enough to guarantee you will get what you want. No time when you'll be 100 percent sure that you're ready to have a child, fall in love, take a job, move cross-country, build a business, show your work, stand in your truth, pursue your dream. Still, at some point, imperfectly informed, with butterflies in your belly, you'll still need to act. To own your unknown. To step into Joseph Campbell's abyss and therein discover your treasure.

Experience and emotion dance in that space. It's where possibility finds its wings. The greatest creations, the most legendary relationships, the most treasured and heralded experiences, innovations, works of art, and lives have all come from people who were willing to live and act in the face of uncertainty long enough for greatness to emerge.

But how do you step into that space, make decisions and take actions there? As I shared earlier, living in the unknown challenges most people. Acting in the face of uncertainty triggers the fear center in our brains. Electrical impulses and chemical agents go coursing through our bodies, making us physically and emotionally uncomfortable. Anxiety, self-doubt, and fear of making the wrong choice compound those feelings as we spin doomsday scenarios of judgment and rejection. A near-perfect chemical, electrical, and emotional storm rains down upon us. We're wrecked and we just want it to end. So we pull out. We kill the source of the pain, but along with it, we close the door on possibility. This was my life for a lot of years.

I've gotten pretty much everything I've always wanted in life. But as my mom once told me, we shared the same karma. We'd always end up in the winning column, but there would be sustained suffering along the way. I've been an artist, an entrepreneur, and a maker of things my entire life. I was born to create a lifetime of somethings from nothings, but the process, living perpetually in the question, often gutted me. I began to wonder if that was really just my karma, or if there was another way. Why did some people seem to handle the massively uncertain quest to create great art, enterprise, relationships, and lives with so much more ease? Why could they walk into a sea of uncertainty unfazed, while others—most people, in fact—ended up a quivering puddle of anxiety? Was it genetic? Were these people just freaks of nature? Or was it trainable? And if it was trainable, how?

This, in fact, became the central question in my last book, *Uncertainty: Turning Fear and Doubt into Fuel for Brilliance.* Turns out that a very thin slice of humans *are* just wired for ease in the face of uncertainty. Most of us, though, are not, including many of the most extraordinary creators of our time. How do they live in the unknown long enough to do amazing things, tell gorgeous stories, and craft lives of deep meaning and impact? Do they all suffer maniacally in the name of possibility? Do they consider that to be the cost of a life fully lived?

Some do. Others self-medicate with everything from drugs to shopping, but it turns out there is another way. You can train yourself to find grace in the space. To cultivate the ease needed to first survive and then thrive as you move through the abyss and into the extraordinary. To not die a death of a thousand doubts along the way.

How? Funny enough, the answers have been right in front of most of us our whole lives. They are far simpler than you may have expected. Three words: *mindfulness, movement,* and *story.*

We've talked about mindfulness as a way to cultivate aware-ness. There is another aspect of the practice that makes it a power-ful ally in your quest to befriend uncertainty. It teaches you how to let go. All those doubts that fill the space of uncertainty can paralyze or even make you ill. Mindfulness teaches you to zoom the lens out so you're able to more easily identify when you're spinning doom and gloom, and then do one simple thing. Let it go. Maybe not the first time, or the hundredth or even the thou-sandth. Over time, the practice grows into a mindset. The process of dropping the stories that shut you down and coming back to the space of possibility becomes an increasingly persistent state of being. I'd love to tell you I've reached that place, by the way. I'm not fully there yet, but I've been able to find so much more grace in the space over the past few years as my own practice has deepened.

Movement is the second uncertainty power tool. We've already talked about movement and exercise in detail on Vitality Day 2—Make Exercise More Fun Than Sex. For now, know that a growing body of research has made it crystal clear that movement is as much for your brain as it is for your body. The angst and anxiety that often accompany action in the face of uncertainty can be greatly diminished by regular, intense exercise. Move your body, ease your mind.

Story is the final tool in the box. When we enter a place of uncertainty, we tend to start spinning stories that predict failure endlessly in our heads. We need a way to hit PAUSE, then consider a different story. One fueled by possibility rather than defeat.

Mindfulness lets us recognize the spin cycle and begin to pull out. Movement resets our brains, allowing for a more optimistic state to reign. Then it's up to us to envision the story of success as vividly as we've spun the story of failure. These three tools become a power triad in the quest to live in the question long enough for life's greatest moments, awakenings, connections, and experiences to become our realities.

Daily Exploration:

Step 1—Create your perfect moment.
Take a few moments and ask, "What would I love to do or create or have that I'm not pursuing because it's not a sure thing?" Write your answer in your journal. Then ask, "What would my life look and feel like, how would it be materially different, if I got what I wanted?" Journal your answer. Now ask, "What am I waiting for?" Write it out.

Chances are pretty good that the thing you're waiting for—the sign from God, perfect moment, or bit of information—will never come. Or it will come only after you've taken some action to step into the quest. So what one thing might you do to stop waiting around? Not some time down the road when the stars align, but right now? Yes, now. Write it down. In the next 24 hours, take that step. Then, the next day, take another, and another. The perfect moment is the moment you choose to act.

Step 2—Use your tools.

If you have not yet begun your mindfulness or movement practices, check out those chapters now and get started. Mindfulness is a slow medicine, and it will take some time before you feel its ability to lighten your journey through the unknown. Movement, however, has both fast and slow mechanisms. It rewires your brain over time but also has a much more immediate "intervention" effect, often within minutes. This is why many of the top CEOs and creators in the world now treat their daily exercise practice as sacred. It's what allows them to stay sane under the weight of sustained uncertainty.

Step 3—Change your story.

Mindfulness gives you the ability to zoom the lens out and more easily distinguish between circumstance and story. It enables you to look at an experience that rattles you and ask a few questions that put you more at ease, even if there is no more certainty to be had in the moment. What are those questions?

- What's the worst that might happen?
- How likely is it to happen, really?
- How would I recover if it did happen?
- What might I learn that would put me in an even better position moving forward?
- What's the most likely outcome?
- What's the best possible outcome?

Answering these questions helps shift your focus from the unlikely and often paralyzing doomsday scenario to a more optimistic and realistic set of stories that fuel both greater peace of mind and the sustained action that leads to better outcomes.

DAY 8

take A FOREST BATH

As I write these words, I'm sitting in an old, overstuffed chair on the balcony of a beautifully renovated barn in Woodstock, New York. It's 5:45 A.M. My family and, it seems, the world have not yet risen.

Massive, hand-hewn beams form a wooden lattice that soars 30 feet up to support the raw cedar planked roof. Three feet to my left, a set of French doors stands open. Cool morning air sifts through the screen and pours across my lap, while birdsong commingles with cicadas and the occasional croak of a bullfrog rises from the pond at the end of the field. A wash of trees, green with joy, rustle their leaves, embracing the barn and climbing up the side of a nearby mountain.

Thoreau's beautiful reflection on the intimate relation between nature and life in *Walden; Or, Life in the Woods* comes into my mind:

I went to the woods because I wished to live deliberately, to front only the essential facts of life, and see if I
could not learn what it had to teach, and not, when I came
to die, discover that I had not lived. I did not wish to live
what was not life, living is so dear; nor did I wish to practice resignation, unless it was quite necessary. I wanted to
live deep and suck out all the marrow of life . . .

There is something about nature, and woods in particular,
that changes us. I grew up in a suburb of Manhattan that served
as the inspiration for *The Great Gatsby*'s East Egg, where our house
sat on a corner lot. One road led to the bay, the other to a small
stand of trees with a network of hidden trails and the occasional
burst of raspberry bushes. I would often bounce between the two.
The beach was my place to "come down" when things got bad at
school or home. The trees were my secret place to get away and
refuel. I never questioned either. I just knew when it was time to
head off to one or the other. Sometimes with friends, but most
often alone.

It's a habit that I've actually kept to this day. I live in Manhattan now, surrounded by the madding pace, the never-ebbing
calamity of people, planes, sirens, and cranes, the frenetic, breathless energy and nonstop overstimulation that defines a city where
the world alights to "make it." Yet, two blocks west, the Hudson
River awaits. Three blocks east lies Central Park, the size of a small
town itself. It is without a doubt the city's greatest invention and,
very likely, the only thing that makes the borough remotely livable.

On any given day, you'll find me secreting away to one or
the other, most often a thickly wooded area in the middle of the
park called the Ramble where the city falls away. Blindfolded and
dropped into the right spot, you'd think you'd been spirited into
the middle of a nature preserve miles from humanity (though, I
have to admit, it does get its fair share of humanity in the summer
months). Small creeks meander among towering maples and one
of the richest diversities of flora ever assembled. I walk into these
woods nearly every day, find a small perch, and just sit. Breathe.
Notice. When I walk out, life is better.

Turns out the Japanese have a phrase for this, *shinrin-yoku*. It literally translates to "forest bathing." Japanese culture has been hip to the intimate relationship between people and nature for millennia. But in 1982, the head of the Japanese Forest Agency wanted to inspire people to improve their health by spending more time in nature, so he coined the term *shinrin-yoku* and launched a government-sponsored campaign to encourage it. The program and the phrase exploded into the Japanese public's consciousness in 1990 when, as detailed in Eva Selhub and Alan Logan's book, *Your Brain on Nature*,[11] Dr. Yoshifumi Miyazaki of Chiba University conducted a series of experiments that tracked and analyzed the effects of *shinrin-yoku* on people's brains, physiology, and moods. Since then, follow-up studies on more than 1,000 people have confirmed the benefits. On a subjective level, people experience increased happiness and pleasure, improved sleep and energy, and a calmer, more relaxed state of mind. But it turns out there are also profound changes in physiology that lead to these felt experiences. Lab tests on the forest-bathers revealed:

- Reduced brain blood flow in areas that signal anticipation of stress and anxiety

- Improved heart-rate variability, a marker for resilience and circulatory health

- Increased immune response, especially in the prevalence of "natural killer cells," antiviral cells, and anticancer proteins

Translation: *shinrin-yoku* doesn't just make you feel better, it alters your physiology in a way that makes you healthier and happier and potentially helps fight disease, infections, and cancer. Interestingly, these effects remain even a week after the forest-bathing experience ends. How and why it works is still up for debate, but one possible contributor lies in a chemical secreted by certain trees called phytoncides. These compounds are connected with improved immune function, and in the Japanese experiments, the levels of phytoncides measured in the air correlated closely with the beneficial outcomes.

But it's not just about what's in the air, and you don't need to immerse yourself in thousand-year-old forests to get much of the benefit of nature. Turns out even the smallest exposure can help. As Selhub and Logan detail in *Your Brain on Nature*, even seeing nature through a window or having plants in a room or in view makes a very real difference:

- In a work setting, anger, depression, anxiety, and fatigue dropped by 40 percent over three months just by having plants in view, and stress plummeted 50 percent. Over the same period, stress in those who went plantless actually rose by 20 percent.

- Postsurgery patients recovered faster and required less pain medication.

- Prison inmates with views of nature had far fewer infirmary visits, as did kids in classrooms that had been "greened" with potted plants.

Simply put, nature is a big, bad bundle of Vitality Bucket–filling love. It affects nearly every important marker of physical and mental health. And, more important, on an experiential level, it's just plain awesome. When I come back from the wilds of Central Park in the late afternoon, or from a walk along the mighty Hudson through one of its lush parks, everything feels different. Also, on a creative level, the pause produced by stepping away from my work inevitably ends up making space for a near-endless parade of amazing insights and ideas to arrive. That, in turn, ends up filling my Contribution Bucket.

So maybe it's time to create your own version of a greened-up space or a daily forest bath. Time to tap a bit of nature to elevate your mind and body and fill your Vitality Bucket.

Daily Exploration:

Let's make this really easy to digest. You may be thinking, "But I don't have an ancient forest or a beach down the block."

No worries. As you've discovered, even the smallest addition of greenery can make a big difference. So today I'm going to offer a few options to make sure that, no matter where you are, you'll be able to join in.

Option 1—Greenify your living and working space
Buy a few small plants today and place them in view, ideally within a few feet of where you spend much of your day. Of course, if you feel like having a bit more fun and you've got the space, add a bit more and create your own green inner sanctuary.

Option 2—Take a nature bath or shinrin-yoku
Find a place with a lot of green. It can be woods or a park or even just a block with verdant lawns and trees. Even if you live in a city, there's a good chance that somewhere there's a little park or community garden where you can walk or sit in a more natural environment. As you walk or sit, let go of the thoughts spinning in your head and just hit PAUSE. If at all possible, leave your phone behind or turn off notifications. Tune in to your senses. Breathe in the air and notice how it feels, what it smells like. Don't just look, but see. Really take in the details of the environment, the colors and textures. Listen intently. Who and what do you hear? Feel the temperature, humidity, breeze, or any other sensation. Spend a minimum of 15 minutes in this place. If possible, see if you can grow that window to 40 or more minutes over time.

If you'd like a little audio guidance for your "noticing" practice while you move through nature, I've recorded a short and sweet guided audio that you can download for free at goodlifeproject.com/bookinsider.

DAY 9

UNFIX your MIND

Watching the scene unfold, as a dad, was on the one hand fascinating and on the other hand incredibly frustrating and sad. Two kids, maybe 10 or 11 years old, were playing a game together. Round one, the kid on the left soundly trounces the kid on the right. Round two, same thing, though the kid on the right does a little better. Halfway into round three, it's getting obvious that the kid on the right is on a path to losing yet again. This time, instead of finishing the game and taking the hit, he cuts it short, proclaiming, "This sucks. I always hated this game anyway. I wanna do something else."

Truth is, this is not just about kids playing a game. I'm guessing you've seen this same scene unfold with adults in nearly every part of life. In fact, it's a safe bet we've all *been* that kid on the right at many moments in life. And there's a good chance we'll be him again.

It's all about what happens when things stop coming easily. Maybe it's the wall we hit at work, when we go from cruising and feeling like we're in our element to having to do something that, for the first time, feels brutally hard and takes more than we've ever had to invest. Could be a relationship, where we reach a moment or conversation in which, for the first time, we don't have all the answers and are forced to figure it out. Maybe it's the craft or pursuit of art or performance. We hit a point where things start to feel a lot harder. We keep trying to find a way through, and when it doesn't come easily, instead of leaning into it, we stop trying, we stop taking risks and start to blame everyone and everything but ourselves. It's rigged. The equipment or tool or computer or fill-in-the-blank is inadequate. It's impossible; nobody can do it. That person is brutal, evil, impossible to deal with, doesn't listen. It's stupid. They're stupid. I really don't care, anyway. I've got better things to do.

We stop attempting anything that's not within our realm of talent, where we're more or less guaranteed not to fail. We walk away from more and more of life's invitations to evolve, grow, and rise. Excused on the outside, defeated on the inside. But we'll never let anyone know.

How we deal with those moments, when things stop coming easily and we need to work like we've never had to work before to make it through, is a big factor in our ability to get what we want out of life. Those moments will always come; there is no part of life that is immune. Stanford professor and author of *Mindset: The New Psychology of Success*,[12] Carol Dweck, has spent decades researching exactly what happens at these points of resistance. Focusing mostly on students in the beginning, she wanted to understand why some kids cruised through those points with ease and continued to grow and improve, while others ended up dejected and defeated.

Turns out it wasn't about intelligence or any of the other things we usually think about. It wasn't that the smarter kids had an easier time finding a way through. The higher-intelligence kids, in fact, were just as likely to crash and burn as any others. Actually, it was often the so-called gifted and talented kids who had the hardest time. How could that be? What was really going on?

The answer is critically important, because moments of adversity, when things get hard and you need to be able to push through, rather than run, exist in nearly every part of life. If you run and hide every time you bump up against one, you end up closing the doors to what are often the most beautiful, though challenging, parts of life. Somehow, we need to be able to find a way to move through these points of resistance and make it to the next level of success, in pretty much all areas of life. But how?

Dweck's research revealed something astonishing. Your capacity to stay with and eventually triumph when things get hard is less about innate ability and more about whether you believe success comes from talent or effort. If you believe that success comes from some innate gift, something you either have or don't have, you very often end up faring worse. You're more likely to back away and make excuses when things get hard. This makes sense. If success is about talent, the moment things stop coming easily, you translate that as hitting the limits of your gift. Whatever talent you might have has taken you to where you are, but you've used it up. Pushing harder won't get you anywhere. Working harder won't do anything. You've done what you can with what you have; now it's time to move on.

Not only is this untrue, but it also tends to be a mighty tough pill to swallow, especially if you've assumed the identity of someone with a certain gift and presented yourself publicly as such or built a reputation around it. So instead of saying, "Sorry, people, my gift won't take me there," you make excuses, rationalize why it doesn't make sense to try anymore, and walk away. Dweck calls this the "fixed mindset," the belief that success is powered by some inborn talent that has a natural cap.

If, on the other hand, you believe that success is more about effort than talent, when those same difficult moments arrive, you take a different approach. You see them as opportunities to learn and grow. Your job is to figure out how to embrace the trial, continue to work hard, explore new ways of moving through it, and ask for help from teachers, mentors, and guides. Though it may still require serious effort and assistance, you're more likely to view the challenge not as a blockade, but as a test. It's not a signal that you're at the end of your road, it's an opportunity for you to go deeper, try harder, do something different, ask for help, innovate and learn. So you do.

That lens, which Dweck calls the "growth mindset," combined with the effort it fuels, leads to growth rather than defeat in the face of adversity. It leads to sustained evolution and a willingness to lean into, rather than run from, all the many challenges that'll come your way. It lets you experience moments of challenge as gateways to possibility. As Dweck writes in *Mindset*, "stretching yourself and sticking to it, even (or especially) when it's not going well, is the hallmark of the growth mindset. This is the mindset that allows people to thrive during some of the most challenging times in their lives."

That leaves us with a question. What's your mindset? Fixed or growth? And if it's fixed, can you change it?

According to Dweck, we're all a blend of fixed and growth mindset. You may have an immediate sense of your orientation. When I was younger I had a much more fixed mindset, but in my later years I've become far more growth-minded. I believe that talent matters, but when it comes to success in nearly all parts of life, effort and a willingness to ask for help are far more determinative. In the exploration below, I'll share some of Dweck's questions to help you figure out where you are on the spectrum today.

If you're strongly growth-minded, awesome. Keep on keeping on. If you find that you lean more toward the fixed mindset, the good news is that the growth mindset is largely trainable. In fact, just knowing about the difference often spurs a change. We'll explore a few ways to move into more of a growth mindset in today's exploration. Keep in mind, though, as Dweck so powerfully shared in her September 2015 article in *Education Week*,[13] that "the path to a growth mindset is a journey, not a proclamation." Do the work, but give it time.

Daily Exploration:

Step 1—Are you more fixed- or growth-minded?
You may already have a pretty solid sense of your view on challenge and growth. If not, Dweck offered some great questions to consider in an article in *Education Week*. When you come up against challenges, she asks:

- Do you feel overly anxious, or does a voice in your head warn you away?

- Do you feel incompetent or defeated?

- Do you look for an excuse?

- Do you become defensive, angry, or crushed instead of interested in learning from the feedback?

- Watch what happens when you see [someone] who's better than you at something you value. Do you feel envious and threatened, or do you feel eager to learn?

Dweck also suggests that you consider how you handle criticism. Does it make you react in any of the ways described above? These are all signs of a fixed mindset. On the other hand, if you experience challenges and criticism as opportunities to learn, grow, get better, move to the next level of success with anticipation and excitement, you're more likely to lean toward a growth mindset.

Step 2—Train the growth mindset.
If you find yourself more on the fixed mindset side of things, all is not lost. With practice and time, you can train yourself to become more growth-minded. So much has to do with the way you frame challenge in your mind and the way you speak to yourself.

Over the next 24 hours (and hopefully beyond), any time you find yourself thinking, "I'm not good at this, I can't do, I don't have the capacity to [fill in the blank]," add the word *yet* to the end. Remind yourself that your ability to do almost anything is about your willingness to invite, engage with, and learn from challenges and tests. The faster path to improvement and success is to embrace rather than run from adversity. Think about every opportunity to do something you can't yet do, to learn something you don't yet know, as a gift. A success catalyst.

You may well crash and burn. You may struggle. You may need to ask for help. People may see all of this. But you'll also learn and grow in ways you never imagined. And you'll do it exponentially faster, instead of remaining trapped and limited in all parts of life by your fear.

Remember, the thing you strive for isn't perfection; it's not the easy win or the avoidance of failure. It's the gift of growth, the opportunity for evolution. Life in a box is not life well lived.

DAY 10

take the slow LANE

Is it just me, or is life moving at an insane pace these days?

Back in my lawyer days, I worked in a mega-firm where our offices were spread across two big towers. The senior partner I was working with was high up in one tower and I was high up in the other (though not as high as he was, of course). In order to get from my place to his, I had to go down the hall, out to reception, wait for the elevator, take it down to the lobby, walk to the elevator bank in the second tower, ride up to his floor, then walk down the hall to his office. He was also of a generation that never turned their computers on. Just wasn't his style. In-person was the only way to work with him.

We had been working on a huge project that was on a ridiculous deadline. I was a securities lawyer, so we were always on deadline, taking companies public, launching ventures, merging stuff together and breaking other stuff apart. The stakes were always very high. That's why people hired us. We did the impossible and didn't screw it up. Apparently, I never got the memo on that last part.

I was working crazy hours and living in that weird space where time seemed to slow down one moment, then scream forward the next. As we neared our delivery date, I began to move faster and faster. Thing is, I was still pretty junior. I needed a ton of guidance and sign-offs from the partner on every word, edit, tweak, and suggestion. That meant riding the elevator down, then going across, up, back down, across, and back up, again and again and again. That cost me precious time and forced me to move even faster.

The pace started to get to me. I had become a living, panting bundle of hyper-productive anxiety. Or so I thought. In truth, not only had the pace killed any semblance of joy in the process, but it also started to destroy the quality of my work. I began making mistakes. The faster I'd go, the more mistakes I would make. That became amplified by the fact that I often didn't find out how off track I was until I made the elevator run to the other tower, where someone who knew what he was doing could tell me to do it again. Then I started forgetting things. I'd ride the elevator down and up with a new set of documents, ready to be approved, only to have forgotten the last page. Back I would go. Faster. I'd rework the documents, type faster, think faster, drink more coffee, even pee faster (yup, possible), and then make the elevator run. Still not right. Gotta go faster. Too much to do, too little time. Must. Be. Perfect!

At some point, I just stopped and sat (okay, maybe I actually collapsed, and chocolate may have been involved) and wondered: What the hell am I doing?

The maniacal pace had extracted every atom of joy from the experience, crushing me mentally and even physically. It had also cratered my ability to create on the level that made me feel good, proud, and capable. It made me feel like I was no longer making a meaningful contribution; I was just screwing up. So I hit PAUSE and tried a little experiment. I called it my "hair on fire minus one" experiment. That, by the way, was back in the days when I had hair.

I realized something. The faster I went, the more mistakes I made, forcing me to go that much faster to first make up for the mistakes and then get back on track. It was creating a gutting, nonproductive downward spiral. I was miserable. What if, I wondered, I did the exact opposite? What if every time I felt the pull to speed up, I actually slowed down? Not a lot, just enough to feel like I could do my best work, make fewer mistakes, *and*—maybe most important—return to a pace at which I could be just a touch more present and enjoy the adventure as much as possible. I sensed intuitively that a slower pace would make me both happier and better at what I did.

Every time I caught myself running and panting and freaking out, I'd hit PAUSE, literally say, "Bring it down," then dial back the speed just enough to feel better. It worked. I started delivering better work and enjoying the process so much more. And all I did was make the smallest tweak.

Derek Sivers, founder of CD Baby and legendary nice guy, shared a similar experience recently on his blog.[14] He had been living on the beach in Santa Monica, California. A few times a week, he would grab his bike and ride the 15-mile out-and-back oceanfront loop. Pushing fiercely, Sivers would go as fast as he could, "really full-on, 100-percent, head-down, red-faced, sprinting." He would finish, wiped out and always in about 43 minutes. A few months in, his rides were getting less and less enjoyable and leaving him feeling trashed, so he decided to try an experiment. Instead of head-down, 100-percent brutal, he would just chill out, enjoy the ride, and go at about half his original effort. First time out, he had a great time. He was "relaxed, and smiling, and looking around. Not red-faced . . . barely giving it any effort." He saw dolphins swimming in the ocean, and a pelican flew over him. That alone would have been a major win. But when he checked his watch, he got a huge surprise:

> When I finished, I looked at the time. **45 minutes.** What?!? How could that be? Yep. I double-checked. 45 minutes, as compared to my usual 43. So apparently all of

that exhausting, red-faced, full-on push-push-push I had been doing only gave me a **4%** boost. I could just take it easy, and get **96% of the results**. And what a difference in experience! To go the *same* distance, in about the *same* time, but one way leaves me exhausted, and the other way rejuvenated.

We so often complain about the insane pace of life, the maniacal speed and busyness that sap our vital energy and keep us from enjoying each moment. We try to rationalize it, saying, "I've got enough stuff for three people. Of course I need to pack my schedule and run through life at a breakneck pace. Sure, it's brutal. It's making me miserable. I feel like I can't breathe half the time. I can't stop. But until they figure out human cloning, how else am I going to get everything done that needs doing?"

How else, indeed?

What if all the things that need doing aren't really the things that matter? (More on that in another chapter.) And what if the better, more enjoyable way to get what matters done is not to speed up, but to slow down?

It worked for me. It worked for Derek. Could it work for you?

Simple truth: fast and busy are a choice.

We choose to go fast and be busy because we think it'll get us what we want. All too often, it doesn't. Fast and busy makes life brittle. It makes us feel like every inch of space in life is locked in and there's no room to move. Instead of unlocking productivity and potential, it throttles both. It deludes us into feeling like we're getting more done faster, but in reality, we could get the same done in the same or less time with more grace by dialing it back, not forward. In the end, we're left feeling dissatisfied and helpless to extract ourselves from the process. Except we're not. It's all an illusion.

Brittle, fast, and busy are not what life has given us; they're what we have given ourselves. With the rarest of exceptions, they are often more destructive than constructive. As Sivers shared at the end of his essay, "Much of my effort apparently wasn't effort at all, but just ineffective stress added on top of something to make it *feel* like I'm doing the best I can."

Maybe it's time to hit pause and try an experiment. What if, instead of speeding up today, you slowed down?

Daily Exploration:

First, look at your to-do list for the day (or tomorrow, if it's the evening). Ask yourself, what really matters? The upcoming chapter on that theme, "Know What Matters," will help you make the call. Then ask yourself what you can say no to. You'll find specific guidance on this in another upcoming chapter, "Practice the Loving No." Next, run this experiment. For the next 24 hours, slow down. The moment you find yourself running, hustling, panting, freaking out, forgetting stuff, making mistakes related to speed and busyness, STOP!

Breathe. Shift gears. Change lanes.

Make a choice to slow down, even just a bit. Notice what's around you. It's almost guaranteed that you can bring it down a beat, still get everything that matters done, and find so much more space and grace along the way. As with everything in this book, I'm not asking for blind faith. Try it on for size. Then take a few minutes to write down how it went in your journal. Share it with your Good Life Project buddies. Most important, remember, with the rarest of exceptions, speed and busyness are choices. If you don't like the way they feel, choose differently.

DAY 1

DISCOVER your SOCIAL SET POINT

There's a wonderful moment that Susan Cain, New York mom and author of *Quiet: The Power of Introverts in a World That Can't Stop Talking*, describes in her book. In her early teens, she shows up at summer camp for the first time with a suitcase stuffed not with mementos and forbidden snacks, but with books. She'd grown up in a house filled with scholars. Family time most often meant sharing a room together, reading, or studying quietly. She loved the idea of group solitude. It was in her DNA. Quiet, intimate settings were home. Summer camp, she figured, would be the same, just with more kids, all devouring books quietly in the bunks. Oy!

Cain and I are wired similarly, as are about a third of all adults. I love to be onstage (though there was a time it made me vomit). Questions after a keynote are the most enjoyable time for me. The conversation, the emotional and intellectual exchange and opportunity to connect and help problem solve in real time—it all leaves me breathless. It's like I become someone else. Still, the moment I'm done, I want to run. I'll often look for a door back-stage that allows me to sneak off onto a side street and just spend a bit of time walking alone. If there's water or nature nearby, all the better. If I have a hat, it's on. If I'm in a hoodie, the hood's up. Glasses, a must.

It's not that I don't like people; I love people. Let me qualify that: I love being around the right people, in the right way, *at* the right time, *for* the right time. What gives? I am an introvert. I never really understood that word until Susan broke it down for me. Introversion and extroversion, she said, isn't about whether you're antisocial or terrified of people. It's not about whether you're the life of the party or you have the ability to work a crowd. It runs deeper than that. It's far more complex and, simultaneously, quite simple. It is about whether being around larger numbers of people fills you up or empties you out.

For me, when I step offstage, much as I've loved being with the crowd, I am running on fumes. The experience leaves my energy tank on zero, and the thought of moving into a room to work it for another few hours is gutting. I spent years warring with that inner knowledge, until I realized there's nothing wrong with me. It's okay to be with myself and to do what I'm here to do in the way I need to do it. Susan's book was a big part of that realization.

Filling your Connection Bucket isn't just about finding and building relationships with the right people; it's about doing it in the right way. Setting, context, and volume play a big role in that. I'd rather go deep with one person on the side of the room than flutter from person to person, ensuring I don't miss a one. I'd rather enter a room quietly—reading the energy, the players, and the vibe, taking my time and easing my way in—than burst in with an entourage and create a stir. I'd rather hang out with a small group of close friends over dinner and spend a fair bit of time in solitude than club-hop with a crowd. In college, I spent nearly every Thursday to Saturday night in dance clubs until 4 A.M. They throbbed with a sea of people elbow-to-elbow on the floor, and I loved it—because I was the DJ, mixing beats in the safety of the booth. My headphones gave the further cue that I was in my special place; everyone else should just go and dance.

I'm what Cain once described to me over a quiet lunch as "selectively social." I love people. I'm just selective in both the who and the how. Knowing this, and knowing it's okay, not something that needs to be changed, has been incredibly freeing. Though I'd believed for the majority of my life that my social orientation was something to be fixed, turns out we introverts have some pretty awesome stuff to offer when we're allowed to operate in our natural state. There is nothing to be cured, only something to be cultivated and embraced. Find the right people, then find or create a way to be with them in a setting and context that allow you to leave feeling filled up, rather than emptied out. That's how the Connection Bucket fills.

Chances are, if you are a strong extrovert or introvert, you already know your orientation. Extroverts are most likely to immediately know and stand fiercely in their orientation, because society validates and encourages extroversion as *the* pathway to success. Extroverts want to be seen as extroverts, the ones with the golden ticket. Introverts often hide their wiring in the shadows. They know, deep down, that's how they're put together, but life has told them it's something to be fixed, so they keep it hidden and often try to fight it. They fake extroversion for short windows of time in an attempt to be "normal" but end up spent.

This is more than a bit tragic, because as Susan Cain so beautifully reveals, the power and possibility and potential to contribute associated with an introverted approach to the world is stunning. Far from being a disadvantage, it is a gift. To unwrap the gift, though, you first need to accept it. If that's you, now would be the time to stand in your bad, quiet self.

There's a third category of people who fall somewhere in the middle: ambiverts. And no, those aren't animals that can breathe on land and in water (though I have met a few humans who've made me wonder). Your social orientation is less a check box than a sliding scale, with extrovert on one side, introvert on the other, and ambivert (a blend of both) in between.

You may find you're strongly to one side or somewhere in the middle. In any case, knowing your social orientation is important in your quest to fill your Connection Bucket. It lets you better understand what types of social settings will allow you to flourish, both personally and professionally. It helps you understand which people and conversations will fill you up and which are likely to empty you out. It also gives you a much better sense of how to move into and out of social situations, how to connect with and step away from people in a way that leaves you feeling energized and connected, rather than gutted and disconnected.

I used to work the room after I spoke because I thought that's what I had to do. I'd agree to attend mixers the night before or right after. I don't do that anymore. Instead of meeting friends out at bars or clubs, my wife and I invite a small group over for a slow, meandering dinner together. If I'm scheduled for a large event or gathering, I make sure to also schedule and even map out "escape routes" that let me do what I call social pulsing and refueling, being in the middle of a crowd one moment, then walking in the woods or reading in my room the next.

Now it's time to explore your social wiring.

Daily Exploration:

What's your social orientation? Reading this chapter, if you're strongly introverted or extroverted, chances are you immediately self-identified as such. If so, write it down. Then say, "I own this."

Most extroverts build substantial parts of their life around the ability to fill their tanks with people fuel. I've found there's often less shifting of the way they move into the world when they honor this. Introverts, though, often tell different stories, trying their best to be extroverts. If that's you, here's your permission slip. Just stop. Think about the commitments you have coming up that involve a social element and ask, "Does this fill my tank or empty it?" If it empties it but the commitment is firm, plan a recovery window immediately after, when you can fill your tank with solitude or quieter, more intimate connections. And if the commitment is changeable, think about how you might alter the dynamic to allow yourself to still achieve whatever outcome was intended by the gathering, but in a way that's better aligned with your social set point.

If you don't have a strong sense for whether you're introverted or extroverted, you may be closer to the middle, ambivert part of the sliding scale. That means you'll likely have the ability to be a bit of a chameleon, the life of the party sometimes and wanting nothing more than to read in the corner at other times. Honor that, too.

If you want to go deeper into this exploration, I cannot recommend Cain's book strongly enough. *Quiet: The Power of Introverts in a World That Can't Stop Talking* was a game changer for me. While there is no one definitive test I'm aware of that tells you exactly how much of an introvert, ambivert, or extrovert you are, Susan and her team have now developed a simple online tool that gives you a pretty solid, science-validated answer. You simply respond to a handful of questions in about 60 seconds, and voilà, you're done. You can find it, along with many insightful resources, at quietrev.com/the-introvert-test.

DAY 2

Find Your People

A few years back, I found myself alone in San Francisco with an evening to fill. I called a few friends, some of whom had met, and others who hadn't. Seven in total. That night, we found ourselves at a table in a wonderful restaurant in the Mission. We opened a few bottles of wine, our host paired them with a bit of food, and our quest quickly became to close the place down. "Don't ask; just try it" became the guiding ethic as the chef-de-cuisine curated a parade of edibles that seemed to tumble endlessly across the table. Seats rotated, bellies filled, and connections took root that have since grown into deep, life-affirming friendships. We did, in fact, close the place down.

As we filtered out to the street, nobody wanted to leave. It wasn't just the dinner, but a profound sense that something more real than normal had just happened. A deeper connection. That in this place, in this moment, with these delicious people, we belonged. We were with *our* people. While the evening eventually did come to a close, the energy of that night, the fabric we wove, remains very much intact across all our lives, save one. Tragically, in the summer of 2015, we lost one dear friend, Scott

Dinsmore, in a freak accident on Kilimanjaro. It was a loss we all felt deeply, in no small part because we'd felt so connected. There is, of course, a reason for this connection. One that transcends the glow of sumptuous food and good wine.

Human beings are hardwired to belong. We are innately social beasts. Without belonging, we feel isolated and lonely. We all feel that here and there. That's normal. When it becomes your life or your belief about your future, though, the effect can be devastating, as University of Chicago professor and director of the Center for Cognitive and Social Neuroscience, John Cacioppo, wrote in *Loneliness*. Your IQ and problem-solving abilities take a serious hit, taking self-control along with them and making you more susceptible to everything from binge eating and drinking to all sorts of risky behavior. Raise your hand if you've ever tried to eat or drink your way out of being lonely. Loneliness can contribute to a litany of health problems, from accelerating the progression of Alzheimer's to blunting your immune system and state of mind, rivaling the destructive effects of hypertension, obesity, smoking, and inactivity combined. Like it or not, we are psychologically and physiologically wired to find and be with our people. That, of course, brings up the million-dollar question.

Who *are* our people, and how do we *find* them?

We've all had the experience of being invited to a club, organization, dinner, cocktail party, or other gathering where people surround us, yet we stand there, devastatingly alone. There is no one way to find belonging. No one formula. Nor do genetics and circumstance guarantee you'll find what you need within the embrace of your own family. Having pored over the rich body of academic research on belonging, spent hundreds of hours on the topic with teachers, and built a number of tightly connected communities, both on the ground and in the digital ether, with dozens to tens of thousands of participants, I've seen a few strong guidelines emerge.

Belonging begins with safety. There needs to be an understanding, either explicit or strongly implied, that this is a place and a relationship where you feel safe enough to be the real you. Where you can drop the facade and be seen, heard, felt, and embraced without judgment or demand for change. This, in fact, is maybe the single most important thing we focus on when developing programming and experiences for Good Life Project. We know we are going to ask people to get real, to be open and vulnerable. If we don't make it clear that the "container" we're creating is a safe place to do that, it's game over. So we work fiercely to ensure that, beyond anything else, participants feel safe. That alone has had a near-magical effect on the speed and depth of relationships and the deep sense of almost familial (not the dysfunctional side) bonding and belonging that's unfolded. We've seen people from all walks of life, all ages, all faiths, and all locations become astonishingly close, simply because they found a place to be real together and not be judged. It starts with safety.

Belonging is also about shared values and beliefs. The thing that launched Good Life Project was my "10 Commandments of Epic Business," which was really just a simple set of values and beliefs about how to contribute to the world. Shortly after, I published what I called my "Living Creed," a collection of 35 beliefs that expanded upon the original seeds.

DON'T TRY TO BE DIFFERENT, OWN THE FACT YOU ALREADY ARE.

BE *fierce* WITH YOUR TIME, BUT *generous* WITH YOUR HEART.

PRESENCE, NOT PRESENTS. The biggest wall you've gotta climb is the one you build in your mind, you don't need a hammer to knock it down, JUST THE WILL TO ACT.

FIND AWE, let it SHAKE you, MELT you, LIFT you, then *share it.*

RITUALIZE THE MUNDANE TO MAKE ROOM FOR THE BRILLIANT.

HAVE A STRATEGY, *but be open to serendipity,* THE BEST THINGS IN LIFE ARE RARELY PLANNED. LIFE IS A STORY, if you wouldn't read the one you're telling, WRITE A DIFFERENT ENDING.

GENIUS BEGINS WITH A BURNING QUESTION, *what's yours?*

YOU WILL NEVER HAVE PERFECT INFORMATION, ACT ANYWAY.

IT'S MORE IMPORTANT TO CHOOSE THAN TO CHOOSE RIGHT. *Don't confuse genuine peace of mind* with the PASSING LACK OF ANGST that follows the demise of a dream but precedes a mounting wave of regret. EASY IS NOT ALWAYS RIGHT.

EMBRACE THE THRASH. Uncertainty is a signpost of possibility.

When you align WHAT YOU DO with WHO YOU ARE, YOU'LL BECOME WHAT YOU NEED TO BE.

BUILD A TRIBE, PEOPLE MATTER.

Love so deeply it cracks open the world. HUG PEOPLE HELLO, THEN HOLD ON TO THE ONES WHO DON'T RUN FOR THE HILLS. SERVE OTHERS, BUT DON'T LIVE YOUR LIFE THROUGH THEM. Expose your soul, *vulnerability* is a gateway to strength.

///////////////////////// PAUSE OFTEN, LISTEN DEEPLY.

MOVE YOUR BODY, FEED YOUR BRAIN.

Lighten up, if you can't laugh at yourself, others will happily do it for you.

The quest to create something from nothing is a wholly irrational act, **DO IT ANYWAY.** Lean into the abyss, do the thing that scares you most.

CREATE, DON'T REPLICATE. ════════

FAILURE IS ONLY FAILURE WHEN IT DOESN'T MOVE YOU FORWARD.

CHOOSE GRATITUDE OVER GREED.

A GOOD LIFE ISN'T A PLACE AT WHICH YOU ARRIVE, it is a LENS THROUGH WHICH YOU SEE and create your world.

Rise up. Be your own guru. **THIS IS THE BIG SHOW.**

MAKE MEANING.

This document is posted prominently on the Good Life Project website, which announces, "This is what we're about, if you feel this way, too, come play!" So when some 350 people get on planes, boats, trains, buses, and automobiles from around the world to gather at Camp GLP once a year, they're coming in no small part because they see the world the way we see it. They want to be around others who wear the same glasses with the same-colored lenses. And they trust that we'll create the safety to allow them to let their hair down and be embraced for who they are. The age range of campers, by the way, is 18 to 78, with the biggest spike in the middle years. Many people show up alone, having traveled from different countries, nervous as all get-out, but excited. That's how strong the yearning to find and be with your people is. It's a trust we don't take lightly and an experience that's led to lifelong stories and amazing friendships and collaborations.

Added to safety, shared values and beliefs are often shared Sparks, as I call them—deep interests that inspire you to invest effort for no other reason than the love of the quest. (We'll talk a lot more about this in the chapter called "Spark Yourself.") People often come together around shared fascinations; shared interests in particular questions, topics, or activities; or shared desires to serve a particular person or community. The feeling of connection and belonging often arises not just from the sharing of a Spark, but from the experiences, stories, and knowledge that unfold around shared Sparks. Crafters, for example, develop an entire language and culture, complete with mythology and shared struggles, experiences, and aspirations around a particular craft. Belonging based on the Spark of faith often integrates nearly all the elements we've explored—safety, shared values and beliefs, shared Sparks—in a very powerful way, along with answers to many of life's biggest questions.

Another frequent contributor to a sense of belonging is a common history or story. That may be based on geography or ethnic background. It may be based on faith or friendship. Basically—sometimes for better, other times for worse—we often feel a stronger sense of belonging among "people like us." You might define *like* in some of the ways I have above, but that likeness could also come from simply having grown up in the same town or part of the world.

Before we dive into today's fun exploration, we need to talk about two things, technology and cults.

First, technology. Over the last five years, a huge portion of connection has moved onto the Internet, mobile devices, and apps. We'll talk a bunch more about what that is and isn't doing to us and our ability to connect in the chapter entitled "Look Up!" But for now, just know this: belonging is a dish best served in person. It can and often does start through technology, but there's a connection that is formed when you're face-to-face that changes and deepens everything. It's partly about the real-time nature of conversation, partly about being able to see people's faces and bodies, partly about the human need for contact and sensation. We could look at the research, but honestly, we don't need to. You know this. I've built intentional communities for decades now, from sweaty yoga shalas to global tech-enabled tribes. They are all amazing, but nothing touches the depth of belonging that is cultivated when hearts, souls, and bodies come together in the same space at the same time. And that brings us to cults.

I've been asked, over the years, what the difference is between a deeply connected group with a strong sense of belonging and a cult. The answer, at least in my mind, is straightforward. When I build communities, I focus on exalting individuality, building individual autonomy, and embracing not just the tribe but everyone who matters outside it, in service of everyone. Cults do the opposite. They strip individuality and autonomy and isolate their members from anyone outside the group, almost always in service not of the members or the world beyond it, but of the leader. In belonging to any group, it's not unusual to be asked to give up a token bit of autonomy and embrace a common language or symbology. You see this in clubs, associations, sororities, and fraternities. The question you always need to ask when thinking about belonging to a new group is whether the value of what you're being asked to give up is exponentially exceeded by what you're going to get in return. If the answer is yes, lean in. If it's no, run like hell.

That leads to today's fun task.

Daily Exploration:

Whether you leverage technology to find your people, then build deeper connections, or you create your own local friends and communities, the invitation is simple. Act. Reach out. Embrace your geeky, dorky, eccentric, playful, funny, vulnerable, weird self and find people who share your worldview or your love of movies, books, activities, or anything else. It may not be fast. It may not be easy. It may lead to rejection or discomfort along the way. But it will add to your life in a way very little else will.

Think about groups or activities where you might find:

- The safety you need to be you
- Shared values and beliefs
- Shared Sparks
- Common history/stories

Make a list of those groups or places on a piece of paper now. If you already have them in your life but haven't been so diligent about participating in them lately, recommit. Now you know how important they really are. If you haven't found them yet, now you know the key qualities to look for, so start looking. Make a list of five experiences or groups or activities to try. Then schedule the first one.

One last thing. It doesn't need to be a formal group. You may well be able to find the sense of belonging you need among a small group of friends or even one other person. Don't think you need an entourage to belong to. One amazing soul can do just fine, and often does.

Of course, I'd be remiss if I didn't also remind you about our wonderful Good Life Project Community, which you can join at goodlifeproject.com/community. It's a warm and wonderful place to find your people. To cultivate relationships in a safe environment around shared values, beliefs, sparks and more. As our global online community grows, we've also seen something wonderful happen. Relationships that began online are going local, with members organizing regular gatherings in cities and towns around the world to deepen friendships, form alliances, partnerships, collaborations, and more. So come on over when you have a moment and say hello.

DAY 3

CULTIVATE COMPASSION

"I am angry and sad," Kelvin Moon Loh's Facebook post began. "Just got off stage from today's matinee and yes, something happened. Someone brought their autistic child to the theater."

Loh was in the Broadway cast of *The King and I*, and a mom came to see the show with her son, who was apparently autistic. During an intense moment Loh described as "the whipping scene," the child yelped and then, according to reports, became inconsolable. Loh wrote, "His voice pierced the theater. The audience started to rally against the mother and her child to be removed. I heard murmurs of 'Why would you bring a child like that to the theater?'"

I've heard stories of Broadway performers breaking the fourth wall to admonish audience members for offenses that ranged from cell phones ringing to talking and even coughing. This was, by all accounts, far more disruptive. Audience members raged against the "offenders" until finally, against the child's pleading to stay, they left. How dare this mother ruin their experience!

The first two lines of Loh's post seemed to tee up a coming tirade, building on the audience's rage. Indeed it did. But not in the way you might think. He continued:

This is wrong. Plainly wrong. Because what you didn't see was a mother desperately trying to do just that [calm her son]. But her son was not compliant. What they didn't see was a mother desperately pleading with her child as he gripped the railing refusing—yelping more out of defiance. I could not look away. I wanted to scream and stop the show and say—"EVERYONE RELAX. SHE IS TRYING. CAN YOU NOT SEE THAT SHE IS TRYING???!!!!" I will gladly do the entire performance over again. Refund any ticket because—

For her to bring her child to the theater is brave. You don't know what her life is like. Perhaps, they have great days where he can sit still and not make much noise because this is a rare occurrence. Perhaps she chooses to no longer live in fear, and refuses to compromise the experience of her child. Maybe she scouted the aisle seat for a very popular show in case such an episode would occur. She paid the same price to see the show as you did for her family. Her plan, as was yours, was to have an enjoyable afternoon at the theater and slowly her worst fears came true.

In a comment to his post, he added that, as the lights lifted for the curtain call, he saw the seats where the mother and child had been. Empty. He was heartbroken. "I want her to know," he wrote, "that she is brave and should continue to champion her child. . . . I will continue to make theater for her. And that is the best I can do for now!"

That is compassion. The ability to step outside our self-interest, stand in another's shoes, feel that person's suffering and want to do something to make it better. Empathy meets altruism. It is, quite possibly, the key to human existence and the answer to much of the violence, strife, and separation that seem to increasingly define the world we inhabit.

If you had the ability to see others as you see yourself, to feel their burden, their suffering, their pain, the weight of their history, would that not soften your view of their behavior? Would it make it more difficult to stand on the sidelines while they suffered in defeat or pain or crisis? Would it make it harder to be the source of pain in another's life? Of course it would. Which is why, as a species, we're all born wired for compassion. Our brains have special cells called mirror neurons, which respond, when we see others act and feel, as if we were experiencing and feeling the same thing. This physiology may also provide a bit of a scientific underpinning for compassion's constituents, empathy and altruism. Empathy is the trigger that makes us want to help. So we do. Then the well-documented "giver's glow," an emotional bump in happiness and well-being from helping (we'll talk more about this in the "Give to Glow" section), completes the circuit and makes us want to do more. In this way, if we're really being honest, altruism is never truly selfless. We benefit from the feeling it creates in us. That's okay. The net effect is still the same. More love. More connection. More elevation. Everyone wins.

Sadly, though, we've also come to learn that while compassion and its ingredients can be deepened with practice, they can also be diminished by neglect, also known as life. Empathy, in particular, can be significantly reduced or lost over time. The way society and, in particular, technology are going, the natural process is tending more toward stripping than building (more on the tech piece in another chapter).

We see the effects of this in the alarming growth of bullying in the lives of our kids, in the random shootings and unspeakable violence against adults across the world. You cannot treat others with the force of malice and violence and prejudice we're now seeing unless you first lose the ability to view them as human. Unless empathy has left the building. That's exactly what's happening, and it's not just on a global level. It's in your own backyard. On line at the checkout. In the classroom. At home with the family. In the theater. In the middle of the day. At a matinee in Manhattan, where presumably cultured, educated adults would turn against a mom who was brave enough to advocate for her child and risk being shamed out of a theater.

We are at risk of losing a very real piece of the empathetic core that makes us human. I've heard it said, "But the world today has too much pain. If you took that all on, if you really opened your eyes to it, life would become unbearable." There is great truth in this. And it hints at the profoundly amplified state of suffering in the world today. We each have to find the right balance, to wade into empathy and compassion in a way that allows us to feel, but without becoming consumed and paralyzed by the weight of the suffering. One thing I know. I'd rather live with the weight of empathy than hide in the fallow of indifference.

Thankfully, cultivating empathy, altruism, and compassion has become a field of great interest and academic study. We know, now, that there are concrete practices, things we can do every day, to build our capacity for empathy and compassion. In Buddhist tradition, there's a simple meditation practice known as *metta*, or loving-kindness. It's nondogmatic; anyone can participate and benefit. It's also been widely researched and proven to increase not only mood, but empathy and altruism. It makes us more compassionate.

A 2013 study led by psychologist and neuroscientist Helen Weng at the University of Wisconsin–Madison showed that a simple, daily loving-kindness practice not only increased empathy, but also made people more altruistic. In the study, one group listened to a simple, 30-minute audio that guided them through a loving-kindness practice every day for two weeks. A control group spent the same amount of time listening to a different type of audio, also for 30 minutes a day for two weeks. The results were astonishing. The loving-kindness group became nearly twice as altruistic as the control group.

Loving-kindness practice, it turns out, not only helps build the capacity to feel, but compels you to help and also seems to fortify you with the strength to do so without becoming trapped under the weight of another's suffering. Compassion, Weng showed, is not just an orientation or a stable trait. It's not something we either have or don't have; it is a skill we can learn. Maybe the most surprising outcome, too, is that it took only two weeks.

You may already be someone who walks through each day radiating compassion. If that's you, keep on with your compassionate self. Keep feeling, connecting, helping. The world, even if that's just your close friends and family, will be better for it. Your Connection Bucket will brim over. If you're feeling like you could use a bit more compassion in your life, the good news is that we now know it's trainable. In today's Good Life Exploration, I'm going to let you investigate your own loving-kindness practice.

Daily Exploration:

Practice loving-kindness meditation.

In loving-kindness practice, you repeat a few simple lines in your head, each time making a different person the focus. A simple script for this practice might have you starting with the thought "May I be free, may I be happy, may I be healthy, may I live with ease." After a few minutes of repetition, you then bring to mind someone you care deeply about and replace *I* with that person, while visualizing them and directing the verses and their intentions toward that person. A few minutes in, you swap in a third person as the subject of your thoughts, someone you don't feel any specific affinity or aversion toward. Then you move on to someone with whom you feel a sense of struggle. And finally, you make *all beings* the subject of your repeated intentions.

It seems so simple, yet it is incredibly powerful. I integrate the practice into my morning routine a few times a week, and I've found that, on the days that begin with it, I tend to move through the day feeling more connected and appreciative.

As with any meditative practice, it's easiest to begin by being guided, so I've created a guided loving-kindness meditation audio for you to download over at goodlifeproject.com/bookinsider. This is not the only way to practice. I have been guided through many nuanced variations. In my experience, the more important thing is the basic intent and the progression of the subject. When you have a moment, head over, download the audio, find a quiet place, and listen. Then spend a few minutes journaling. Write down what came up (this one often brings things up) and how it made you feel.

DAY 4

Look Up!

When was the last time you went to the bathroom without your phone? C'mon. It's just you and me. Tell the truth. Better yet, when was the last time you went to the bathroom for the sole purpose of checking your phone? Good news, bad news: you're not alone. In a 2015 Verizon study of more than 6,000 people, 90 percent said they use their phones in the bathroom.[15] A 2015 Survey Monkey inquiry revealed that 44 percent of respondents have heard a toilet flush on the other end of a phone call. Can I get a collective "Ewww"? And the problem runs much deeper than stolen bathroom time.

With nearly five billion mobile phone users in the world, more people with access to cell phones than toilets in India, and 77 percent checking their phones before anything else in the morning,[16] we've got a problem. We spend so much time looking into our own palms, we've forgotten what it means to look into one another's eyes. Even worse, we don't care. Eighty percent of us are offended when someone we're talking to stops to use their phone, yet an even higher number, 82 percent, still check their phone while talking to someone else, knowing that behavior is offensive. They. Just. Can't. Stop.

MIT professor Sherry Turkle, author of *Alone Together* and *Reclaiming Conversation*, has studied technology and behavior for decades. When I spoke with her about cell phones, she hesitated to use the word *addiction*, arguing it's not like an addiction to drugs or alcohol where the source of compulsion plays no constructive role in our day-to-day existence and can be eliminated without detriment. Connective technologies, and smartphones in particular, are a fully-integrated part of our culture and lives now, like it or not. Along with the bad, there is also great good. But that's not what defines whether a behavior is addictive. Just because the answer is moderation and choice, rather than abstinence, doesn't mean it's not as addictive as any other compulsion-forming behavior or drug.

Make no mistake, we are all living in the hyperconnection matrix. Frantically searching for the next hit of images and texts, updates and tweets, chats and swipes, hashtags and likes. That satisfies a certain need. It makes us feel like we're in the know. We're not missing out. We're connected. On a superficial level, it's true. But on a deeper level, it's delusion piled on top of digits. Digital interaction isn't the same as being face-to-face. We lose something when we replace real-time eye contact and breath with asynchronous images and text. That thing, according to Turkle, is empathy. Without it, we lose both the ability to cultivate compassion and the impetus to help others. That is a bad thing. For us and for civilization.

Funny enough, even the presence of technology kills real conversation. Simply having a phone on the table or within reach keeps conversations shallow. None of this would be a big deal if mobile and app-based conversation were complementing rather than replacing face-to-face conversation, but that's not the case. In fact, so many people are turning to digital to have potentially messy and emotional conversations in a less messy and emotional way. It may bring more calm to a relationship, sure, but it also strips the vulnerability and revelation that come from looking someone in the eye, seeing how your words land, seeing how their body responds, hearing the catch in their breath, understanding what is truly going on between you in a way no emoji chain or composed text could ever express. That emotional, messy, hard, exhilarating, don't-know-what's-coming-next space is where the moments that make life most worth living lie. Kill the space, kill the moment. Hello, tidy matrix and numbed-out life.

Rolling breathlessly from one digital dopamine hit to the next isn't a sign of being alive and informed. It's not a sign of being connected and engaged. It's a sign of being a digital junkie. You are no longer in charge, just like the 82 percent of people who know they're offending those they're with by checking their phones but just can't stop themselves. What do we do?

Abstinence in the world we live in is tantamount to social exclusion. I'm a realist; I get that. Mobile devices and apps are here to stay. I use and love both. At the same time, if we take abstinence off the table, that leaves us with choice and moderation. Maybe it's time to choose differently. Maybe it's time to own the fact that the thing we sought as a conduit to connection has inadvertently become a potentially dehumanizing force. Much as it connects us to the world and keeps us in the know, it also wields the power to disconnect us from deeper conversation, empathy, understanding, emotion, and the kindness that arises out of these feelings and experiences.

So here's my invitation for this week's daily exploration.

Look up!

Just for a moment, remove your head from your apps.

Daily Exploration:

1. Don't walk-n-check.

For the next 24 hours, keep your phone in your pocket while you're walking or standing anywhere. Yes, even while waiting in line. The harder it is for you to do this, the bigger a signal that you need a "phonetervention."

2. Leave your phone in another room with notifications off during meals.

If you're a digital native, you likely don't even consider the possibility that checking during meals or conversations might be rude. Or you follow what Sherry Turkle calls the rule of three: as long as three people at a table are looking up, you're allowed to look down. For one day, try being the person who is always looking up. If it's impractical to have your phone either off your body or somewhere unreachable, then, at a bare minimum, keep it in a bag and turn off notifications. Yes, I know it's hard. And you will live. Special note: if you truly have something urgent that you have to be "on call" for, like a wife in labor or a critical job option that will require you to pick up or miss out, of course you can make exceptions that are legitimate, so you can carry out this exploration in a way that honors its spirit but keeps you feeling okay.

3. Call someone.

Wait, but didn't I just say to put it down? I want you to do something very strange with your phone. Something you may rarely do anymore. Turns out your phone has a hidden function. Not many people know about it, but in an emergency, you can use it. It's called, wait for it . . . a phone. You can actually use your phone to call and speak with people. For real! Pick one person who would normally be on your text list today and, instead, put on your headset, dial their number, put the phone in your pocket, and kick back and talk.

As always, take a few minutes at the end of the day today to journal how it all went, what you noticed, and what you learned.

DAY 5

THE 60-minute LOVE BOMB

It started on Instagram. Mandy Len Catron saw a friend's post about a show at a local art gallery. It looked like fun; she was in. Another friend, who was more of a casual acquaintance and former student, suggested they go together. Cool, she replied. It was a date. Or something. You never really know these days.

They walked around the show for a bit, circling and wondering what was going on, more in friend than first-date mode. Afterward they found their way to a nearby bar and started chatting. As a writer, Len Catron had covered love in a pretty public way and was at ease with the topic. People knew that. She would often find others opening up to her about all things relationship. This night would be no different, but it would go places she never imagined. And she would end up doing as much talking as listening.

Her friend offered a theory; he believed that, given a few basic commonalities, pretty much anyone could fall in love with anyone. He had no idea what those commonalities might be or how to *make* it happen. Mandy wasn't sold on the idea. They were both coming out of relationships that hadn't worked. Then she remembered something. She had spent years studying the topic of love, both as a writer and as an academic. In the course of her research, she had come across a study by Arthur Aron,[17] a professor at the State University of New York at Stony Brook, that fascinated her.

Psychology students were divided into pairs, a heterosexual male and female, previously unknown to each other. Students who disagreed on any strongly held beliefs before the pairing were not matched. One by one, they were brought into the lab and asked to sit across from each other. Over the next 45 minutes, they read and answered a series of 36 questions that became increasingly revealing and required deeper levels of self-disclosure, vulnerability, and trust. At the end they sat quietly, staring into each other's eyes for four minutes. Immediately after, Aron asked them more questions. The results were eye-opening. After just 45 minutes, 30 percent of the students rated the relationships they had just created as "closer than the closest relationships in their lives." Many more stayed close afterward. And to cap things off, six months later one of the Aron pairs got hitched and invited the entire lab to the wedding!

Len Catron shared Aron's experiment with her friend at the bar and mentioned how she'd always wanted to try it. He said, "Let's do it."

"Now?"

"Now!" So they did. There, in the middle of a bar, they found the questions online and passed a phone back and forth answering the 36 questions. Everything vanished away as they moved deeper. Forty minutes turned into hours, as the crush of the bar enveloped them. By midnight, they had wrapped up the final questions. Still, they had one more step. They walked outside to a bridge near the bar and stood, gazing into each other's eyes for four minutes. For Len Catron, that single moment was actually more vulnerable and powerful than the hours of questions that had come before. Or maybe it was *because* of the questions that came before. Shortly after, they began dating and fell in love.

Mandy shared this story in an essay in the *New York Times* entitled, "To Fall in Love with Anyone, Do This."[18] The article became a massive, viral sensation. Millions of readers, it seemed, were looking for a fast track to romantic love. They thought they'd found the elixir in Aron's 36 questions. I saw something else. Diving into his work, I realized romance was not the real subject; intimacy and friendship were. It was more about companionate love than romantic love. I began to wonder what might happen if I tweaked his approach and used it as a tool to rapidly create deep friendships among strangers. To increase the likelihood of people falling in "friend love." Lucky for me, I had the perfect lab to run that experiment.

For a number of years, our Good Life Project team has run an accelerated personal growth experience called the Good Life Immersion. It starts out with a long retreat, often in a foreign country. We often take over an entire boutique retreat center so that we get an immersive, 24-7 experience. We learn together, play together, eat together, and sleep together—well, not like that, but you get the point! People come from around the world. Very few, if any, know each other before we begin. We do a lot of growing during our time together, but from the standpoint of the team, our biggest goal is to create a container that is safe and deliver a series of experiences that cultivate deep trust, openness, and lifelong friendship. People may come for the knowledge and the experience, but it's the depth of the relationships that will sustain them for life. We've been pretty successful at this, but having been exposed to Aron's work shortly before the Spring 2015 program was set to begin in Costa Rica, I saw an opportunity.

I called together the faculty and shared the research, then offered my idea. I should note, I offer a lot of ideas, not all of them good. So I count on my team to keep me in check. What if we modified the questions to keep the progressive self-disclosure and vulnerability, I said, but make them more applicable to our group? Then, what if, every night before sending people off to hang out or go to bed, we gave them a set of questions to answer in small groups. Each night, the question would require them to dig deeper and share more. The team lit up. They loved it. So we did it.

While I cannot provide any hard data, I can say that the outcome blew all of us away. That group was our most diverse ever— ethnically, culturally, spiritually, geographically, and sexually—so there was a lot of opportunity for misunderstanding and division.

Yet by the time the retreat ended, it was like one beautiful family. Shields lowered, facades dropped, hearts and minds opened. Deep, emotional conversations took people into the wee hours of the night. Many, many tears were shed and a metric ton of laughter and revelation forged profound ties in a remarkably short period of time. Was it all about the questions? Of course not. There was so much more going on. But from where I sit, it made a very real difference. It's not an intimacy cure-all. It's not a magic love bullet or spoken-word aphrodisiac (said in the voice of Barry White). But it is a powerful tool that encourages people to get real and go deep—fast.

Cool thing is, you can try it, too. That's what today's exploration is about.

Daily Exploration:

This will take a bit longer than some of the other daily explorations. Likely closer to an hour than 15 to 20 minutes. I've shared all 36 of Aron's original questions, in the order to be asked and answered, below. Don't look at them yet. Now think of someone you might like to begin a real friendship or even a potential romance with, or a relationship you'd like to deepen. Tell this person you have a fun experiment to do where you'll both get to ask and answer a bunch of questions, from fun and silly to deep and provocative. Invite them to meet you somewhere you'll both be comfortable. Remember, Aron's original study happened in a lab, but Len Catron's real-life experiment happened in a bar and yielded equally powerful results.

When you meet, open the book to the questions below (remember, do not read them before). Ask the first question, let your partner answer, then respond with your answer to the same question. When you're done, move on to the next until you're done, alternating who answers first with each question. The early ones will be pretty superficial, some even just fun, and then they'll get deeper. At the end, you'll sit quietly and look each other in the eyes for four minutes; then, if you want, you can share what the experience was like. Find a time when you can both carve out an uninterrupted hour. Then do it. Afterward, spend a few more minutes journaling about your thoughts.

Here, now, are Aron's 36 questions as they appeared in the original research in three sets:

Set I

1. Given the choice of anyone in the world, whom would you want as a dinner guest?

2. Would you like to be famous? In what way?

3. Before making a telephone call, do you ever rehearse what you are going to say? Why?

4. What would constitute a "perfect" day for you?

5. When did you last sing to yourself? To someone else?

6. If you were able to live to the age of 90 and retain either the mind or body of a 30-year-old for the last 60 years of your life, which would you want?

7. Do you have a secret hunch about how you will die?

8. Name three things you and your partner appear to have in common.

9. For what in your life do you feel most grateful?

10. If you could change anything about the way you were raised, what would it be?

11. Take four minutes and tell your partner your life story in as much detail as possible.

12. If you could wake up tomorrow having gained any one quality or ability, what would it be?

Set II

13. If a crystal ball could tell you the truth about yourself, your life, the future or anything else, what would you want to know?

14. Is there something that you've dreamed of doing for a long time? Why haven't you done it?

15. What is the greatest accomplishment of your life?

16. What do you value most in a friendship?

17. What is your most treasured memory?

18. What is your most terrible memory?

19. If you knew that in one year you would die suddenly, would you change anything about the way you are now living? Why?

20. What does friendship mean to you?

21. What roles do love and affection play in your life?

22. Alternate sharing something you consider a positive characteristic of your partner. Share a total of five items.

23. How close and warm is your family? Do you feel your childhood was happier than most other people's?

24. How do you feel about your relationship with your mother?

Set III

25. Make three true "we" statements each. For instance, "We are both in this room feeling . . ."

26. Complete this sentence: "I wish I had someone with whom I could share . . ."

27. If you were going to become a close friend with your partner, please share what would be important for him or her to know.

28. Tell your partner what you like about them; be very honest this time, saying things that you might not say to someone you've just met.

29. Share with your partner an embarrassing moment in your life.

30. When did you last cry in front of another person? By yourself?

31. Tell your partner something that you like about them already.

32. What, if anything, is too serious to be joked about?

33. If you were to die this evening with no opportunity to communicate with anyone, what would you most regret not having told someone? Why haven't you told them yet?

34. Your house, containing everything you own, catches fire. After saving your loved ones and pets, you have time to safely make a final dash to save any one item. What would it be? Why?

35. Of all the people in your family, whose death would you find most disturbing? Why?

36. Share a personal problem and ask your partner's advice on how he or she might handle it. Also, ask your partner to reflect back to you how you seem to be feeling about the problem you have chosen.

Aron, Arthur, *PSPB* (Vol. 23 No. 4), pp363-377, ©1997 Society for Personality and Social Psychology, Inc. Reprinted by Permission of SAGE Publications, Inc.

DAY 6

find Your FOUR LOVES

Aquamarine eyes gaze knowingly upward and to the left, as if my guest in conversation, author and speaker Danielle LaPorte, is receiving the answer. A smile spreads across her face. We've been huddled in a sun-washed corner of a two-bedroom apartment overlooking Portland, Oregon, in the windmill-capped Indigo building. Closing the loop on a wide-ranging exploration, I've just asked LaPorte what it means to live a good life. "Love," she offers. Then again, glancing back at me: "Love."

A single emotion that people live and die to experience, even just for a moment. It's not quantifiable, brutally hard to describe, the source of irrationality, sacrifice, devotion, elation, revelation, pain, joy, happiness, connection, belonging, humiliation, meditation, condemnation, contemplation, and countless other "-ations." It is at once enduring and fleeting. Everything and nothing.

Love it or hate it, the one thing we can all agree on is that we want love. But what exactly *is* love? Is there only one kind, or is it more of a love mash-up, with different types flowing into each other? Turns out, in fact, there are four kinds of love. C. S. Lewis popularized them in a series of radio talks in 1958, then turned them into a book entitled *The Four Loves*, offering the Greek words *storge*, *philia*, *eros*, and *agape*, which translate roughly to "empathy," "friendship," "erotic love," and "unconditional love." In the years since, love has become a growing field of research, and while we still speak of four types of love, the names and descriptions and understanding of each have evolved.

Companionate love is the love you feel among close friends and, with a bit of luck, family members. It's built upon strong feelings of affection, trust, comfort, ease, and likability, along with shared interests and activities. It's the love that women tend to express toward friends with ease, and men always add the word *man*. As in, "I love you, man." Along with a classic pat on the back, of course. When you feel companionate love, you say you love another, but you're not *in* love with them. It's a blend of C. S. Lewis's *storge* (empathy) and *philia* (friendship).

Compassionate love, Lewis's *agape*, is also commonly known as selfless love, pure love, giving love, unconditional or altruistic love. It's the feeling that emerges when you place yourself in service of another person over time. The love that arises out of caring for another. Caregivers often feel compassionate love for those in their care. Hospice workers, especially, tend to develop profound compassionate love for those they help transition out of this life.

Attachment love, as described by University of Minnesota professor Ellen Berscheid, is the feeling of deep connection, security, comfort, ease, and even need that most often arises as the result of compassionate love offered over a longer period of time. It's the feeling of security that runs from a child to a parent, from a long-term patient to a caretaker, or even long-term life partners. Its effects can be so strong as to make partners who've been through a bitter divorce still feel the need to be physically close and remain in the same neighborhood or even on the same block.

But let's get real. When we talk about love on a day-to-day basis, what we're really talking about (and praying for) is romantic love. C. S. Lewis's *eros*. This is when you're *in* love. It's the love we obsess over and may spend a maddening amount of our lives trying to find. It's about sexual desire, lust, romance, sensuality, and deep affection. You can experience companionate love and romantic love at the same time. Many would argue the best relationships have both—and, truth be told, while we tend to fantasize about the sexy, romantic phase, that deeper, sustained friendship love is often the thing we crave most in the long run. I'm astonishingly blessed to be married to my best friend. But as anyone who's ever had a short, hot relationship has discovered, deep friendship is not necessarily a prerequisite for the sex.

According to Dr. Helen Fisher, Rutgers University anthropologist, research professor, and author of *Why We Love: The Nature and Chemistry of Romantic Love*, romantic love triggers three powerful systems to produce a love-drug cocktail in our brains.[19] The sex-drive system is all about sex, sensuality, and testosterone. Romantic love is all about deeper intimacy; it's played out in the brain's dopamine pathways. Attachment, for those who get there, is about long-term security and is tied to the brain's oxytocin and vasopressin pathways. As much as we know about these pathways, though, we know little about how to trigger them. Therein lies romantic love's dilemma.

Companies and individuals have spent millions on methods, algorithms, and applications to increase the likelihood of finding someone who'll give you that magical and enduring blend. Fisher studied assessments completed by more than 13 million online daters in 40 countries. She found that creative, spontaneous, dopamine-driven novelty seekers—Explorers, as Fisher calls them—tend to be drawn to people like them. Traditional, rule-oriented, serotonin-driven, cautious people—Builders—are also drawn to similar-minded partners. Decisive, analytical, disciplined, testosterone-driven Directors, though, tend to be drawn to Negotiators, people who are more expressive, socially graced, nuanced, estrogen-driven, and compassionate. And vice versa.

While these orientations and natural affinities give some clues as to whom we might fall for, they are, as Fisher readily offers, still subject to a whirlwind of other factors. So we're left with more information, but we're still a long way off from anything resembling definitive answers. Well, we explored one fun and interesting way to cultivate love in "The 60-Minute Love Bomb," and in the next chapter we'll explore how your "love language" might help. But for now, one thing we know is that, in the context of how we spend our time on the planet, love matters. Having people in our lives to love and be loved by changes everything.

For however long it lasts, a moment or a lifetime, when you are giver or receiver, it makes things better. Both in the moment and over the course of a lifetime. Close friends, family, and intimate partners make you happier in the moment and richer over time. And that brings us to today's exploration.

Daily Exploration:

Today we're going to do a little journaling. Think about the four kinds of love:

- Companionate (deep friendship love)
- Compassionate (caregiver/unconditional love)
- Attachment (security love)
- Romantic (sensual love)

Think about what relationships you currently have that might satisfy each type of love. Ask yourself how much you've put into nurturing each type of relationship over the last six months. Write down one thing you might do in the next 24 hours to either deepen an existing loving relationship or begin to cultivate a new one.

In the next two Connection Bucket chapters, we're going to explore two very specific ways to cultivate romantic love, both between existing partners and between you and someone you might love to be in love with (and be loved back by).

DAY 7

WHAT'S YOUR LOVE LANGUAGE?

I've never cared all that much about material things. If it didn't allow me to better perform an activity I loved, it didn't matter to me. Show me a mountain bike that would let me bomb downhill trails, a microphone that would let me record better audio, or a camera that would let me shoot better video, and I'd be all over it. Outside of that, I am just not a stuff person. That also makes me a miserable shopper.

I've often said to my wife, Stephanie, I could live pretty happily with just a handful of possessions and a suitcase packed with old jeans and comfy T-shirts. Shoes optional. That same orientation toward stuff had flowed through my relationships. Stuff, in the form of gifts, has never meant much. The gesture behind them is nice, but in the end, it's just more stuff. In case you're wondering, yes, I am the guy who is impossible to buy things for. I don't want for much.

How does someone show love and appreciation in a way that speaks to me? Touch me. Be with me. I'm not just talking about intimate touch (though, with my one and only, that's always great). I'm talking about physical contact (with people I know, strangers not so much). Hugs among friends, an arm around a shoulder. Kicking back on the couch, reading with my daughter with her legs strewn over mine. A loving embrace. That, and just spending time together doing something we enjoy, undistracted. I've always known this intuitively and sought it out, but I never expressed the need until pretty recently.

Stephanie, on the other hand, loves to give and receive gifts. She loves every part of it. Shopping for gifts is heaven. The wrapping matters. The box, the paper, the bow, the bag, the card. The entire presentation and process of offering. It all matters. She likes the package, the contents, and the pageantry. Where does this come from? We don't really know. When she was growing up, her dad was a gift giver. Himself the son of strong Sicilian parents, he was a deeply devoted, loving man, but also far more stoic than softie. He'd always come home with something for Stephanie. That's how he'd learned to show his love and how she had learned to receive it and, in turn, give it. But when it came to Stephanie and me, there was a wrinkle that took some time to unfold.

We've been together nearly 25 years now, married more than 19. In the early days, Stephanie keyed in on the fact that being physical and doing things together was what I needed. I discovered (with a lot of help) that she loved giving and getting gifts. So we both endeavored to speak in each other's language. To be fair, she did much better than I did. The gift thing took years for me to get. Truth be told, I'm still working on it, and for the life of me I will never understand what makes for a nice bag.

Then something surprising happened. Something neither of us really picked up on until very recently. We've always spent a lot of time together. We now work together full time. We love being around each other, helping each other and creating things together. Working and building a life together is not for everyone, but it is for us. Stephanie still loves to give gifts to others, and she still loves to receive them from others. But between us, it's become less meaningful. It's less a language or a symbol than a nicety. We've both wondered about this. Did my years-long incompetence just finally lead her to give up on my ever being a half-decent gift giver, or was something else happening?

Enter Dr. Gary Chapman, who spent more than 35 years pastoring and marriage counseling. He also says he had plenty of experience working on his own marriage of more than 45 years. In his work, he began to notice certain patterns. People came to him with partnerships in various stages. Many were in disarray. They loved each other, they'd tell him, and they thought they were expressing their love, but it wasn't landing or being received. Instead they felt like they were in relationships defined by love denied or abandoned.

Through his research, Dr. Chapman discovered that people have natural preferences about the way they both give and receive love and appreciation. He was able to tease out what he called the five languages of love, described in detail in his book *The Five Love Languages: How to Express Heartfelt Commitment to Your Mate.*[20] For easy reference, they are:

- Physical touch
- Receiving gifts
- Words of affirmation
- Quality time
- Acts of service

Dr. Chapman has since written many more books that expand the reach of the love languages to different types of relationships.

I had never heard of his work until a friend, Marie Forleo, told me she had been using it in two very different contexts. It started with her life partner, but then she decided to extend her exploration to every employee in her company. She wanted to be able to build a team where each person felt appreciated and loved in a way that would truly land. Marie is one of the most intuitively "tapped in" people I know, so I was inspired to dive into Chapman's work and take the love language test myself. Sure enough, physical touch came out on top, with quality time ever so slightly behind. Receiving gifts, not surprisingly, was at the very bottom. Interesting, the assessment seemed to validate my gut and experience.

I showed my results to Stephanie, and she wasn't surprised either. Then she took the test. Here's where things got interesting. If you had asked both of us to predict her primary love language before taking the test, we both would have said it was receiving gifts. Her results showed the exact opposite. Like me, receiving gifts came out on the bottom. Stephanie's primary love language, at least in the context of her relationship with me, was quality time, followed by acts of service. How could that be? How could we both have been so off?

As we talked it through, things started to become clear. When it came to anyone but me, Stephanie still loved giving gifts. That was how she expressed love. She also loved receiving them. And, in the early days of our relationship, giving gifts was how she wanted me to show appreciation and love. Through her dad, that's what Stephanie had come to see as the face of love. It's what she had come to expect. But as we grew closer over the years, she started to open to the idea that love could come in different ways and deepened into the realization that simply spending time together and receiving acts of service was what she really wanted from me. Would a beautiful box with a pendant necklace make her happy? Sure. But if she were to choose between that and a quiet weekend at a bed and breakfast, she'd take the latter in a heartbeat.

When we walk down the street together now, I almost always sneak my hands into my pockets and I know, within seconds, she'll slide her arm through the space between my elbow and body. It's such a small thing, but I notice it every time, and I love it. If my hands are free, she'll reach out to hold one. Every morning when I rise, I know I have a job to do. Even when I stopped drinking coffee for bit (I've since corrected that sin), I would grind the beans, make a fresh pot for her, and then doctor up a cup just the way she likes it. If we're driving anywhere together, I drive. There's no conversation, it's just the way things are. Small acts of service, offered without the need for recognition, is part of how I show love, and she feels it.

The big common language between us, the one that more or less tied for number one for both of us, is quality time. In the early years, we spent a lot of time trying to figure out what that would look like, what we loved to do together. When we were dating, we'd exercise together all the time. I love mountain biking and used to do it every chance I could get. She gave it a try but soon learned it wasn't her thing. We've taken cooking classes, baking classes, traveled, signed up for weird workshops, gone on retreats, and tried a lot of different things. Some of if stuck; much of it didn't. It's been an ongoing process of discovery that, more recently, led us to work together.

People often ask in disbelief, "Seriously? All day, all the time?" We smile and nod. One thing we discovered is that it really doesn't matter all that much what we're doing. We just love being around each other and building things that matter together. We've ended up, almost without intention, speaking each other's love language with a fairly high degree of fluency. This, we've learned, has been a blessing. It's deepened our relationship, our ability to give and receive love and appreciation. It is very likely a big part of the reason we can spend so much time working together, and not only *not* want to kill each other, but want to then go away together.

Finding your love language, then exploring how that meshes or clashes with those you're in a relationship with, is a powerful ally in the quest to deepen those relationships and fill your Connection Bucket.

Now it's your turn. Do you have a sense of the way you most want to receive love and appreciation? You will in a moment.

Daily Exploration:

It's time to figure out your love language profile. As I shared above, Dr. Chapman's five love languages are:

- Physical touch
- Receiving gifts
- Words of appreciation
- Quality time
- Acts of service

Start by just asking yourself how you like to give love to those closest to you. Answer intuitively. Then ask yourself how you like to receive it. Would you feel more loved and appreciated by a hug or a mug? By a love note or getaway on a love boat?

You may have a very strong, clear sense right away. Still, in light of how Stephanie and I were taken by surprise by our love language assessment, I encourage you to take that same test. Then have your partner and maybe even your close friends take it. It's online, and it's free. It may immediately validate what you already know, or as Stephanie and I discovered, it may initiate a deeper exploration and conversation that lead to a fuller awareness of what you truly need and how it might not have been what you thought. Be sure to not just set the results aside, but have a conversation about it with the one or ones in your life to whom you look to receive and give love. Then spend a few minutes journaling what you might do both to give love in a way that allows it to land better and to provide better guidance on how you want to receive it.

As always, for easy reference, you can find Dr. Chapman's free love language online assessment at 5lovelanguages.com.

DAY 8

DIAL IN to SOURCE

Swirls of incense and patchouli thickened the already musky air as we gathered for an evening of *kirtan*, the Sanskrit word for "devotional music," led by legendary *kirtan wallah*, or "chant-master," Krishna Das, whom we would come to call simply K.D. The room darkened, leaving candles to throw their light against walls thickened with the paint of sweat and liberation. A hundred of us sat on well-worn blankets, some against walls, others with legs crossed, spines rising like serpents and eyes half-closed. We were in a sacred space on Manhattan's East Side that served as home for the students of famed yoga teacher Sri Dharma Mittra. I was not a devotee but had come along for the experience.

A few years earlier, I'd found myself practicing and training to teach yoga and meditation 10 hours a day in a small town on the Mexican coast. With us was K.D. As we eased into Savasana, or final relaxation, after morning practice, K.D. would make his way into a corner of the room and begin to sing, layering a raspy, haunting baritone over the ethereal sounds of the harmonium and waves tumbling onto the beach just feet away. And every evening ended with us sitting together, often into the late hours, as K.D.

led us in the classic call-and-response *kirtan* style. Every word a foreign language, yet somehow deeply ingrained and understood. A beautiful, almost otherworldly sense of profound communion would settle over the room.

I would dip in and out of the flow, sometimes lost in the weightlessness of the moment, other times crashing down into my self-conscious self and retreating to voyeur mode. When I was in it, though, there was no place I'd rather be. That deep knowing that you are not alone. That you are a part of something bigger. Connected. Tapped in. It's not just you. It's not just people. There is a bigger us among us. Between us.

Sitting in Dharma Mittra's New York City studio with years of practice and study and teaching separating that moment from my time with K.D. in Mexico, I was back for another hit. Another evening hoping to reconnect with that sense of oneness that had become more fleeting than fixed in the intervening years.

We all define that experience, that awakening, differently. It's often created through some blend of upbringing, experience, and instruction. Many of us found the essentials through faith and family, through tradition and practice. Others through a moment of awakening or gentle exposure to practices that opened a window over time. Even atheists among us, while disavowing the existence of a being or omniscient entity known in some form as God, often acknowledge that there is a collective consciousness that exists both within and between us. Some even find it in nature: the swell of the ocean or fertile embrace of the forest. Some find it in the shared practice of a craft or the feeling of a pencil on paper, a brush on canvas. However you define that sense of oneness or source, it's the feeling that we are participants in, both beholden to and receiving from, something bigger than just us.

During that magical evening with Krishna Das at Dharma's place, he'd pause often to share stories, insights, and experiences from his life. A rock-and-roller from Long Island and basketball star at Brandeis in his youth, he found himself called to India in the 1970s to study meditation, along with others like Ram Dass. Over the years, he returned there many times. He shared that evening how he was tired and was looking to go again soon. India was where he "plugged back in" to source.

Over the last few decades, at least in the United States, we've seen a wide-scale departure from organized religion, but not so much from the larger sense of oneness or spirituality. In fact, a growing number of people consider themselves spiritual, open to the experience of something bigger, but disconnected from the doctrines and strictures of traditional faith. Demographers have come to call this group the "nones," as in spiritually inclined but unaffiliated with any one religion. Regardless of how you define that etheric sense of connection to source, to something bigger, most people do seem to be wired on some level, across every culture, to yearn for and take comfort in it. We tend to be happier when we live with the sense of both connectedness and surrender that comes from acknowledging that some form of universal consciousness exists and guides our behavior beyond the bodies that carry us through each day.

Does that mean every person must find or deepen a connection to source, in whatever form, faith, or expression feels right to them, as a prerequisite to a life well lived? No. There may well be plenty of happy, fulfilled people who deny the existence of anything smacking of God, consciousness (either individual or collective), source, oneness, or anything related. You don't get kicked out of the good life club if you don't feel it or have any need or desire to experience it. But if you do, if it is something that matters to you and you've found yourself drifting, now might be the time to reconnect. That is today's invitation.

Daily Exploration:

If you are someone who finds solace, comfort, elevation, or grace in the idea and experience of connecting with something bigger than yourself, take a few minutes today and think about a time where you felt most tapped in to that feeling. Where were you? Were you in nature, in a house of worship, in quiet prayer alone, walking in solitude, working with your hands, in meditation, in *kirtan*, singing, volunteering? Who was with you? What were you specifically doing? Paint the picture and describe how it made you feel. Then ask, "When was the last time I felt that way? When was the last time I shared in the activities or community that created this feeling? Can I schedule a time to do more of it sometime in the next week? If so, then how, where, when, and with whom?" Then do it.

DAY 9

VANQUISH the VAMPIRES

Have you ever been in a room with an energy vampire? You walk in and immediately know something is a bit off. No worries; you're an optimist. It'll work itself out. So you begin a conversation. And then you feel it. In every moment, with every word, you feel a little more of your soul being sucked out of your body. Minutes or, if it's been a full-on assault, hours or perhaps even days later, you're left an empty husk. You, my friend, have just been sucked dry by an energy vampire.

Okay, so maybe I'm being a bit melodramatic. But we've all felt what I described. An interaction that, for some reason, leaves us utterly drained. Maybe it's the person who assails you with an idea, asks for your "honest" opinion, and then spends hours battling you in a closed-minded quest to prove how wrong you are. Maybe it's the family member, mired in obsessive pessimism, who refuses to see the astonishing blessing that is his life and chooses, instead, to focus relentlessly on all that is wrong. It could be the narcissist who requires constant adulation to make it through each day, with you as the go-to source of heaped-on glory. There's the boss who takes every opportunity to position herself as superior and piles work on you to keep you in your place. Or maybe it's the person who is really down and anxious, in need of endless amounts of validation and love.

Whatever the source of any one person's energetic black hole, the commonality is a profound neediness. These folks require large and sustained amounts of energy, not just from us but also from the world, to be okay. Often they have no awareness of this dynamic. They're just living their lives, doing what they must to get by, given the deep emptiness that fuels their need to take more than they give. Then, of course, there's the passive-aggressive energy vampire, sucking you dry one moment while giving effusively the next to keep you coming back for more.

It's easy to judge these folks, but to what end? Born to different parents in a different time or a different place, you might've been them. You still someday may be. All too often, this profound yearning is driven by an emptiness, a suffering that none are immune to in life. What if we approached these people from a place of compassion? If, instead of saying, "What an idiot," we asked, "What must she be suffering to need so desperately?" Compassion changes our views on life-sucking behavior. That doesn't mean you just relent and submit. Compassion is just a starting point.

If, as a first step, you come from a place of compassion, you may find you're more forgiving and gentle, less reactive, and more able to create the boundaries and shields needed to preserve your own energy. Then again, you may not. The dynamic may be so ingrained that a better way to stop the energy extraction is simply to step away, to disassociate yourself from the source of pain. Often this is a viable path. Leave a job or a relationship, end a connection, or just functionally turn it off.

But what about those energy vampires you cannot leave?

Find or deepen other relationships that have the exact opposite effect on you. Ones that lift you. Ones that give you more than you could ever give back. Ones that leave you feeling like you've just had a life-force transfusion. I call relationships that serve this role your energy beacons. Having them in your life is critically important. They fill your Connection and Vitality Buckets. They connect and empower you. Beyond your ability to create your own boundaries, they are the ultimate energy vampire hedge. Having energy beacons in your life can be essential when your energy vampire is a close family member, one you can neither walk away from nor hope to change. In those scenarios, think shields up, beacons on.

One final thought. As I've shared, energy vampires often have no idea of their impact on others. All they know is that relationships are hard, people never seem to be able to give them what they need, and they are in a state of constant yearning for validation that never seems to come. There is a hole that cannot be filled. They wonder, "What's wrong with everyone else? Why don't they see what I see? Why do they refuse to give me what I need?" At some point, everyone abandons them, either literally or figuratively, by becoming unavailable and incommunicative, and they have no idea why. The reason, of course, is because it's them, not the world, and life is too short to live in a sucked-dry state.

If you see yourself in the above description, you may be the unwitting energy vampire in other people's lives. This book may help you both awaken to your role and develop the sense of self and meaning and alignment needed to change. But your level of need and behavior may come from a deeper yearning that may be better explored in partnership with a qualified professional.

On to today's exploration.

Daily Exploration:

Today we're going to make two short lists, then do a little journaling together. First, make a list of any people in your life you feel fit the description of an energy vampire. Ask if any of those relationships are loose enough that you'd feel comfortable letting them go. If these people provide a specific need or service that others might provide, can you find someone else to give you what you need without the toll on your personal energy? If so, make that list of replacements and begin the pruning process.

Next, look at who is on your list that you're either not willing or not able to release from your life. Maybe it's an ailing parent who has moved in with you. Or a partner whom you are not open to leaving. Or a boss or colleague who is tied to a job that, at least for the time being, you cannot leave.

Ask how you might be able to find compassion for them and see their behavior in a different light. Then own the fact that, when they behave in a certain way, it's about them, not you. Step back and watch the behavior, more like a detached outsider than an actor in the play. Let it land, and then let it go. Think about ways you might be able to set up shields and buffers, ways for you to extract yourself from as much of their behavior as possible. Can you do what you need to do but be less personally available? I know it's easier said than done, but to the extent you can find a reservoir of compassion to tap into, that can go a long way toward making the situation more livable. It might be helpful here to reflect on the chapter entitled "Cultivate Compassion."

One more thing: commit yourself *fiercely* to doing something every day to fill your Vitality Bucket. The more optimized your mindset, the easier it becomes to stay positive and full in the face of potentially draining interactions.

Now make your fun list. Who are the energy beacons in your life? Who are the people who, for reasons that may be completely unclear, leave you energized? The ones who tend to radiate light that pours through you and stokes your own inner fire. Who are the people who, when you show up drained, leave you full, even if they never say a word? Make that list. How often do you spend time with them? The more vampires you have in your life, the more beacons you need and the more time you'll want to spend with those who fill, rather than empty, your Good Life buckets. Write down ways you might make that happen. Then send e-mails or texts, make calls, and get those dates on the calendar. Now.

DAY 10

UNCAGE YOUR CONVERSATION

For the better part of my life, I was known as "the guy in the kitchen" at parties. Who am I kidding? I'm still the guy in the kitchen, but now I call it cooking instead of hiding out.

Truth is, I've never been the most comfortable person in any room. I'm on the quieter side. I'm not all that confident approaching people or inserting myself into conversations. For a very long time, conversation didn't come naturally to me. In fact, I was awkward to the point of making other people uncomfortable (though that may have just been the perpetual thought bubble in my head).

People who have seen me teaching or onstage are often surprised to hear me say that. I can stand before 1,000 people and tell stories, crack jokes, deliver emotional zingers, or teach ideas, running around filled with energy. When I take the stage, I take on a persona. It's an amplified version of me, a performance, not the one I bring to everyday life.

When I'm in a more intimate setting, I get to just be me. Truth is, the real me is pretty low-key. I tend to move into social situations slowly, whether a dinner party or a meet-up. I don't say much for a while, and yes, I still feel more comfortable in the smallness of the kitchen where I can help out or run the show, rather than be at the whim of the conversation gods.

How, then, does someone like me end up on-air, recording and filming long, in-depth, often revealing personal and emotional conversations with total strangers? Conversations filled with laughter and tears, where we often go where they've not gone before. I've been wondering that myself lately. What I've realized is that, over the last five years or so, I've become much more a student of conversation.

Driven largely by the desire to build relationships with amazing people, learn as much as I can from them, and devise better experiences to share, I've spent countless hours studying the art and craft of conversation. I've deconstructed some of the interview greats from radio and television. I've poured myself into the study of what some call interpersonal or social dynamics, watching, listening to, and observing not just what's being said, but also the 80 to 90 percent of the conversation that happens nonverbally. Physical cues, movement in or out, raised eyebrows, vocal cadence and intonation fascinate me. I've broken down and reworked my own process.

There was also something else that developed over those same five years that made a real difference: my mindfulness practice. It gave me a greater ability not just to know about the subtle cues that unfold between people, but also to notice and respond more intentionally to them. To know when we are in a moment together, where the real conversation is just waiting to surface but needs either the slightest nudge or a bit more silence to manifest.

I began to realize that what I thought was a gift that you either have or don't have was actually something that could be learned. I also began to distinguish between an interview, which I "conduct" for the purpose of soliciting information, and a conversation, which I "co-create," seeking not just wisdom but connection and elevation. Podcast listeners often tell me they feel as if they're listening in on a private conversation between friends. That's what I'm going for. Of course, there's also the occasional person who doesn't get that the format is conversation and not interview and just wants me to shut up!

Somewhere along the way, I began to realize that I wasn't born a conversationalist. I'm still very much a student, but I no longer entirely suck at it. The art and craft of conversation, I discovered, could be learned. Then something really odd began to happen. People started to *thank* me for the conversations we were having. Remember, we're talking about me, awkward kitchen guy. Moments before writing this, an e-mail landed in my in box from a recent guest:

> I've participated in many interviews, but your session is truly extraordinary. . . . What strikes me most is the easygoing tone you created, which yielded a very natural, engaging conversation between the two of us. . . . I was struck by how comfortable we seemed, how often we laughed.
>
> One of the characteristics of great leaders (think: Steve Jobs) is that they help *others* be at their creative best. So thanks for all your great provocations, and for giving me so much room to share my beliefs.

This note came from someone who has built a groundbreaking global organization and now spends much of his life traveling the world speaking and being interviewed.

Even more surprising, without even realizing it, those same skills have begun to work their way into my day-to-day conversations. I was recently at a friend's book launch party. It was wall-to-wall people, not my scene. I usually just hide in the corner at these events. True to form, that's how I began. Then a number of people, many of whom I'd never met, started to find their way over to chat. Old me would have found any reason to exit the conversation. But I didn't. I talked. We talked. It was fun. I realized my biggest barrier now was no longer a lack of skills; it was my dated definition of myself as an inept conversationalist. It was time to start shaking free of that.

Throughout this whole process, I've stumbled upon a few truths. Here is the big one: conversation is the gateway to connection. You don't have to be a ninja, but if you can get down a few basics, your ability to build relationships improves greatly, and so does your life. Those basics can be taught. Below, I'll share some of the things I've figured out and then point you to some great additional resources.

Mindset is key. Cultivating a mindfulness practice has given me the sense of awareness needed to better understand what's really happening in any given conversation. It lets me more easily see the conversation beyond the conversation, which is often far more interesting and far more real. It has also helped me notice when an obsolete, conversationally crippled model of myself is stopping me from just relaxing into what would otherwise be a wonderful give-and-take of ideas, energy, and stories.

If you are at ease around others and find yourself naturally graceful in conversation, that's fantastic. If you feel you could use a few tips that might help you connect with more ease and less angst, opening the door to conversation and new relationships, you're going to have some fun with today's Daily Exploration.

Daily Exploration:

There are volumes of work on building conversation. Here I'll share my top seven tips and invite you to try one, two, or as many as you're inspired to try. Once you do, be sure to return to your journal and write a bit about the experience.

1. *Set your intention to give, not take.* Many people move into social situations looking to get something. Others will smell that on you from a mile away. It reads as aggression and self-interest, even if you don't say a word. A thousand subtle cues telegraph your intent. Before you begin, say to yourself, "How can I serve?" From that place it becomes nearly impossible to leave as a loser.

2. *Give your undivided attention.* Spend more time looking into someone's eyes than you do looking over their shoulders. Undivided attention is such a

rarity these days, people crave it desperately. When it is offered, it is often experienced on the level of a gift. Give that gift.

3. *To be interesting, be interested.* Counterintuitive as it may sound, you don't need to say much to be interesting. You just need to ask the right questions. Most people will find you interesting if you are deeply interested in them. Stop thinking about what to talk about; start thinking about what to ask.

4. *Lead with different questions.* Do you really care about what someone does? Then why is that the most asked opening question on the planet (behind "What's your sign?" of course!)? People want to talk about what they're sparked by. If that happens to be their career, great. But sadly, more often than not, someone's job is not the same as their Spark. Ask questions designed to elicit their Spark. Some starters:

    a. What's holding your interest these days?

    b. What have you read (or seen, or heard, or been working on) that excites you?

    c. So tell me about (subject you know the person cares about).

5. *Ask, listen, pause, and ask.* Once you've asked questions that elicit someone's Spark, stop talking. Let them talk, and just listen. Really listen. When I record conversations, I don't bring a script, and I rarely even have any preset questions. The more scripted I am, the less I listen, the less I hear and see what really matters to my guest, and the less I'm able to respond to moments, ideas, tangents that almost always hold the best parts of the conversation. Don't think ahead to what you're going to ask next. Just listen. When your partner is done, pause for a moment, then respond to what was offered and ask another question. If, after a few rounds, neither of you is drawn in, then either it's not a great

connection or you haven't truly found their Spark, in which case, see item 4.

6. *Notice what's not being said.* The vast majority of communication is nonverbal. Studies have found that words account for only 10 to 30 percent of communication. What makes up the other 70 to 90 percent? Nonverbal cues, like body language, facial expressions, vocal cadence and intonation, breathing, physical positioning. Learn to see and hear not just what's being spoken, but what's being said beyond words. If someone is constantly looking around while you're speaking, you're not holding their attention. Look at their body. If their feet are turned away from you, they're just waiting for a chance to exit. Are they leaning in (engaged), leaning back (aloof), arms open and animated (excited), arms crossed (closed and defensive)? You can study up on so much of this, but truth is, if you just pay attention, people's subtler cues are pretty easy to translate, and they often speak far more loudly than anything they're actually saying.

7. *Practice mindfulness.* You can try out and experience the effect of the above six tips in just a matter of seconds. This final one, though, is a longer-term game. It's about cultivating a mindfulness practice that increases your moment-to-moment awareness of both social cues and your own inner storyteller. We went much deeper into this in the "Wake Up" chapter, of course.

As always, try some of these out, record your experiences in your journal, and if you're inclined, head on over and share what unfolded in the online GLP group. If you'd like to go deeper into understanding and mastering conversation in a much more nuanced way, I've included additional resources for you at goodlifeproject.com/bookinsider.

DAY 1

SPARK YOURSELF

Ever have one of those moments when a deeply held belief is shattered and a new realization floods in? That's what happened to famed *Eat, Pray, Love* and *Big Magic* author Elizabeth Gilbert. The topic was passion.

Gilbert had been traveling the country, speaking, writing, and preaching the gospel of passion. "I would tell anybody who was stuck near me listening," she said. "You had to find and identify that one thing within you that made you feel like your head was on fire, that one thing you would jump off a cliff for, that one thing you would sacrifice everything for, and you had to put every molecule of your being behind that one thing and that was the only way."

Returning home after giving one particular sermon on passion, she found a message from a woman who'd heard her speak.

> "After hearing you speak tonight, I have never felt like more of a loser because . . . I don't have a passion. I don't have one thing that is so clearly everything to me. One thing that I would risk everything for. . . . It isn't because I'm lazy and it isn't because I'm depressed. I've spent my

life tearing myself apart trying to find my one tower of flame that would be the guiding principle for everything to follow and I'm telling you, it's not there. I feel like a freak. I feel like there's something missing from my DNA, and I came to hear you tonight looking for guidance, and you just made me feel like an idiot."

Gilbert was destroyed, crushed, but also grateful for the wake-up call. She thought about so many of the people she most admired and loved in her life. "Many of them have [had] very unusual and convoluted paths on the way to finding where they were ultimately supposed to be," she told me. "And the way they got through all those convoluted, strange mazes and paths was by following their curiosity until their curiosity took them where they were meant to be, which meant sometimes a long and tricky and often painful journey."

Curiosity, she realized, is not only a more realistic predictor of a life well lived, but also a much more forgiving and helpful guide. I've found this exact same thing, both in my life and in conversations with so many accomplished teachers and creators of well-lived lives. At any given moment over the last 20 years, if you'd stopped me and asked, "What is your passion?" I would have answered with a puzzled look and a shrug of my shoulders—even at times when I was deeply curious about and loving life, which has been my near-perpetual state for as long as I can remember.

Ask the average person that same question; you'll get the same deer-in-the-headlights look. The inquiry all too often lands as a conversation-killing judgment bomb rather than a gateway to inspired dialogue and possibility. Framing passion and purpose as both a singular thing and a prerequisite to a life that matters is part of the challenge. But I wonder if there's something more nuanced going on. What if the bigger issue lies in our decision to frame the question using the nouns *passion* and *purpose* as things to be had, rather than using adjectives that describe ways of doing something?

What if instead of asking what your passion or purpose is, we asked different questions? What are you interested in? What are you curious about? What's fascinating to you? What have you read or seen or heard that you want to know more about? What do you love to do, just because? What are you working toward that you want desperately to achieve for no other reason than that you want it? Who do you love to help or serve or lift up?

For many, in an instant, the heavyhearted deer-in-the-headlights look would dissolve into lightness. A long list would tumble forth.

What if you don't so much *have* a passion or purpose as much as you pursue something, or a bunch of things, *with* passion and a *sense* of purpose? And what if the deeper you get into that exploration or pursuit and the more competent you become, the more interested you get in doing and learning and discovering on a fiercer, more engaged, dare I say a more "passionate" or "purposeful" way?

What if it isn't so much about having to find that ever-elusive solitary passion or purpose, but rather finding a way to spark your interest in something that increasingly pulls you from ahead, the deeper you wade into it? With passion. With purpose.

The idea of "sparking," or igniting a level of interest that fuels breathless action for no other reason beyond the intrinsic joy of the quest, came to me from a conversation with Alice Wilder. Wilder develops educational television for young kids. She was on the team that launched the *Blue's Clues* juggernaut and is now a towering force in the space.

Her entry into the field came as the result of two distinct moments she describes as her sparks. Alice's first big spark came during her sophomore year at Skidmore College when a psychology professor turned to her one day and said, "You know, I really like the questions you ask." Until that moment, Alice told me, "nobody had ever said to me that they liked something about the way that I thought . . . and it was in that moment . . . that I got excited about learning." She'd originally gone to school to get a degree in business, but her professor invited her to work in the learning lab, where she was brought into elementary schools and taught how to interview children. She'd always loved kids; their spirits lit her up. But she'd never made the connection to something bigger until then.

While this was happening, a second spark came from a very different place, Hollywood. The movie *Big*, with Tom Hanks, hit theaters. In *Big*, a secret wish transforms 12-year-old Josh Baskin into a 30-year-old adult. He finds his way into a job as a toy tester and developer with savant-like abilities to understand what kids really want; as we the audience know, he's able to tap into his 12-year-old sense of wonder and curiosity and play. But there was one scene in particular that, added to Wilder's recent spark by her professor, changed the course of her life. It was the scene in which, in a boardroom of adults, one toy is being touted as the next big thing. As it gets passed around, Josh, in the guise of an adult, says, "What's so fun about that?"

In that moment, Wilder knew. She wanted Josh's job, but in real life. "I wanted to talk to kids, to be the voice of children in a room full of adults that are making things for kids." A force bigger than her took over and began pulling her to learn more, to master the art and science of getting into kids' heads and translating their words into programming that adults would create for them. She began to pursue her curiosity, love of serving kids, and desire to master her craft with passion and purpose. The way she contributed to the world lit her up, filled her with joy and meaning.

So, how do you spark yourself? I can't say I know the entire answer, but looking into my own life, then analyzing common sparks from hundreds of conversations with accomplished and deeply fulfilled creators like Wilder, I've identified five types of sparks.

1. Curiosity Sparks

Curiosity sparks often come in the form of a burning question, a deep yearning to discover an answer to a problem that, for some reason you may or may not understand, you feel compelled to solve. Curiosity is the spark that led Alice to want to understand how children's minds work and then learn how to translate that into products and programs that light up their rapidly developing brains. It's also the spark that often fuels my business and writing adventures.

I tend to latch onto a question and then spend years in search of an answer. My first book, *Career Renegade*, asked, "How do you earn a living built around something you love to do when there is no conventional path to get there?" My second book, *Uncertainty: Turning Fear and Doubt into Fuel for Brilliance*, asked, "Why do some people seem to handle the sustained uncertainty of the creative process well, turning it into fuel, while that same experience destroys so many others? And what can you do to get better at it?" My current venture, and this very book, ask the ultimate question, "What are the essential ingredients of a life well lived?" The quest to find answers has filled me up, provided a deep sense of meaning for years, and, thankfully, has also become the way I earn my living.

2. Fascination Sparks

Fascination sparks often happen when you're exposed to a topic, an idea, or any other thing that triggers an intrinsic desire to learn. It's not so much about answering a question or solving a problem; there's just something about a topic or thing that fascinates you. You feel like you're wired to be interested in it, and given the opportunity, you'd even pay and devote your most precious asset—time—to learn about it.

Dan Carlin, a former radio host and now producer of the legendary podcast *Hardcore History*, is a fantastic example. From a young age, he's shared, he was drawn to history. It became a consuming fascination that never left him. He found himself wanting to learn more and devoting huge amounts of time to studying it. That led him to eventually transform his fascination into astonishing multi-hour podcasts that take listeners into his story- and research-driven world of history. And apparently he's not alone in his interest, as millions of listeners download each episode and wait, often for months, for the next to arrive.

3. Immersion Sparks

Immersion sparks are generally triggered by activities that make you want to do more, regardless of the outcome and without any quest beyond the simple desire to enjoy what you're doing. Crafting is a great example. From the outside looking in, you might assume that someone sitting at a craft table is driven largely to create a "finished product." And, sure, that's part of the reason why people craft. But there's something bigger going on. The process itself, the very nature of the activity, delivers a big part of the reward.

Interestingly enough, most would view the field of science as one driven largely by a curiosity spark. I mean, it's all about solving a problem, getting the answer, right? That is definitely a big part of the pull. But many scientists are equally (if not more) lit up by the day-to-day process of discovery. As famed physicist Richard Feynman said when he learned of his Nobel Prize award, "I've already gotten the prize. The prize is the pleasure of finding a thing out, the kick in the discovery, the observation that other people use it—those are the real things."[21]

Immersion sparks are engaging activities you lose yourself in, ones you do because the activity or the process alone is the reward. You want to become immersed in them.

4. Mastery Sparks

Mastery sparks are closely related to immersion sparks and are often bundled with them. They are about working fiercely at something not only because you love to do it, but because you are drawn to achieve a level of mastery. It's not just about doing it; it's about getting good at it. How good is a matter of individual choice. Some folks get everything they need from simply reaching a level of competence that lets them feel skilled, able to do or create on a level that lights them up. Others are more fiercely called to higher levels of mastery, to become truly great at something, maybe even the best in the world.

There is no right or wrong here, though the trade-offs involved in pursuing mastery to the point of becoming the best in the world can often lead to greatness in one domain and underdevelopment in all others. So when you find yourself in the grip of a mastery spark, on a quest to be the world's best, stop regularly on the way. Recognize the sacrifice that this level of achievement will almost always require, and make a deliberate decision about what you're willing to give up in the name of mastery.

5. Service Sparks

The final spark I've come across many, many times is the service spark. This is the fire that is lit when you think about serving or helping or in some way giving yourself to a particular person, group, or being. This spark is often bundled with others. Alice Wilder is driven by a deep curiosity about early-childhood learning and the process of creating media. But underlying all of this is a bigger overall spark. She does it all in service of kids. She wants to create an experience that kids love to participate in, while also knowing they'll be learning along the way. She wants to be their voice at a table of grown-ups who all sit in service of them.

Susan Cain, who, as I've mentioned, penned the international bestseller *Quiet: The Power of Introverts in a World That Can't Stop Talking*, spent seven years researching and writing her epic book. Was she fueled by a deep curiosity, a love of research and writing, and the desire to craft an extraordinary book? Yes. But all of that was in service to something bigger: the global community of introverts who represent a third of the world's population, most of whom have been told by society that there's something wrong with the way they're wired. Her book exploded into the public's consciousness, in part because it was extraordinarily well researched and written. But even more, it was profoundly in service. It gave voice to millions who'd spent their lives feeling voiceless and broken and wrong. That book, in turn, sparked millions to learn more about introversion and its relationship to life.

As you've seen, it's not unusual to be sparked by some blend of the "Big 5" at any given time. Here's what's really important to remember: it's okay if no single spark ever rises to the level of all-consuming "mad passion" or "life purpose." More important is just the feeling of being sparked. Lit up and drawn to invest your energy in something that calls from a place within to do more. That mix may stay fairly set for life, or it may evolve as you move through the different seasons of your time on the planet. Either way, you still qualify for a Contribution Bucket–filling, deeply satisfying life.

Daily Exploration:

Time for you to spark yourself! What are the things that you want to invest time, energy, money, and effort to do, learn, or participate in more? Answer as many of the following questions as you can. Truth is, it's often easier to have fewer sparks, because then you spend less time trying to decide which to devote time and effort to. You can still contribute to the world in a way that lights you up.

If you find yourself struggling to answer for present-day you, answer for 12-year-old you. Sometimes by the time we reach adulthood, our true sparks are buried so deep we have forgotten how to see them. Reconnecting with your inner 12-year-old, without regard to whether adult society holds your answers valid, can be a great place to start.

- Am I curious about anything in particular? Is there a big question I'd love to answer? Is there a problem I feel compelled to solve?

- Are there things that fascinate me? Is there a topic or field or thing or pursuit or even a person that I have a deep yearning to know more about?

- Are there activities that I get lost in? Are there things I love to do where I lose track of time and would pay to be able to do more?

- Is there something I want to master? Is there an art or field or pursuit I'd love to be really good at, maybe even world-class great?

- Is there some person or community or being I feel compelled to help? It doesn't have to be human; it could be an animal, a plant, or even a planet.

Look at your answers, then ask how you might be able to weave more of the things that spark you into your days.

DAY 2

KNOW WHAT MATTERS

What do you mean, I have to decide what to have for dinner? Seriously, if I have to make one more decision, I'm gonna lose it!

Every moment of every day, we're bombarded by a freight train of opportunities, people, ideas, invitations, ads, conversations, and asks screaming at us. With every one, we've got to make a decision. Yes, no, maybe, kinda, later, now, bigger, smaller, hotter, colder, cuter, higher paying, less traveling? Taxi, subway, bus, walk, or ride? Single-origin, high-altitude organic coffee with lovingly handpicked virgin hemp milk, half-caf macchiato with 2 percent, or slam a double espresso? By the time we hit breakfast, we're beyond overwhelmed!

Then come the real decisions, the ones that actually matter. Yes, our caffeine transport system matters, but a handful of other choices may actually be more life-and-death, or at least happy life and slow, meaningless decline into death. Little things like who gets our attention, when do they get it, and why? What gets the nod, what gets turned down, and how much will someone need to give us—in money, love, attention, or a sense of purpose—to make it worth a yes? What projects, jobs, activities, and relationships do we welcome, and what do we say no to? How much suffering will we endure, and why, before changing direction?

Make the right decisions and the way we contribute to the world ends up filling our Contribution Buckets. Life gets a whole lot better. So do the lives of those we end up dancing with and serving. Make the wrong decisions, though, and it feels like we get to the end of every crazy busy day but haven't actually done anything that matters. String that out for weeks, months, and years and, boom, we've just wasted the better part of our lives.

Thing is, we can't make good decisions until we know what matters to us. Until we have some sense of what's important, what we believe, what we value. When we know these things, decisions get easier. Something's either aligned with our values and beliefs, or it's not. If it's aligned, it's a yes. If not, it's a no. If we have two options, both well aligned, we choose the one that's a better fit.

Of course, that doesn't mean we never experience angst when saying no to something cool in the name of something that matters more. Or that the answer is always crystal clear. Black-and-white clarity is rare. The seemingly everpresent grip of FOMO (fear of missing out) and its maniacal, ADD-addled tentacles of distraction leave us prepetually wondering if there's a bigger, better job, person, deal, or future out there! Meditation helps, and a daily awareness practice lets you see more clearly, but c'mon, we're all still human. Emotion and irrationality will always have a seat at the table. Which is why it's that much more important to know yourself well enough to be able to make decisions that survive the taunts of the gremlin of doubt.

The more I think about it, the more it seems we don't really have a decision-making crisis. We have a self-knowledge crisis. How can we decide who or what to say yes or no to until we know what matters to us? So let's bypass years of psychotherapy (kidding—many of my closest friends are psychotherapists!) and take a bite out of the self-ignorance apple with a simple question:

What is important to me?

Tough question, right?

There are so many ways to answer. The politically correct way, the nonchalant hipster way, the struggling artist way, the PTA parent way, the L.A. rocker way, the responsible grown-up way.

I'll share an approach that's worked well for me. But first, a big warning: Answer these questions as if nobody's listening. Assume nobody will ever know what you've said. Why? Because if we think our answers might someday "get out," we inevitably end up lying to ourselves. We give some blend of what Stephen Colbert calls "truthiness," or little white reinterpretations of the truth. The moment we consider we might have to share our answers, we default to the way we either "wished" we felt or the way we think we're "supposed" to answer.

Don't do that. Self-knowledge isn't about the person you wish you were or might someday become. Nor is it about the beliefs and values you think society wants you to have. It's about who you are now. As you read these words. Honest, unfiltered, politically, socially, and morally in-the-moment you. Own your truth. Good decisions don't come from self-delusion. They come from ruthless self-knowledge, brutal honesty. When it comes to doing what matters, truth beats truthiness.

Now let's talk about that question "What is important to me?" Another way to put it is "What do I most value?" Same basic question, but it's often easier to answer this way. I recently asked a roomful of people to share the things they value most in life. Here are some of the words they shouted out:

• Faith	• Truth	• Openness
• Family	• Vulnerability	• Wonder
• Freedom	• Equality	• Fun
• Peace	• Integrity	• Growth
• Compassion	• Humility	• Accountability
• Security	• Play	• Kindness
• Friends	• Simplicity	• Justice
• Love	• Trust	• Flexibility
• Respect	• Generosity	• Mindfulness
• Money	• Creativity	• Courage

Then I asked them to look at the list and edit it down to their five strongest values, the ones they'd hold most sacred. Inviolable. The most important things in their lives. Once they had their top five, I asked another question: So what?

What do you do with this information? So now you know family matters or money matters or health matters a lot. But how does that information guide your decisions and actions? Hmmmm. What if we took it one step further and added a verb to each?

Let's take the value of "family" as an example. Okay, so family is really important to you. But just saying that doesn't help you make decisions. What if we changed it to "provide for my family"? Better. Now we've got a verb attached to it, an action. Still, the word *provide* is vague. For one person, it might mean supporting financially; for another, it could mean being present. Even the phrase "provide financially" is vague. And who exactly is included in "family"? Is it just my partner and kids? Is it that third cousin, twice removed, who I see once a decade?

What if we took that word—*family*—and turned it into a sentence that guides how we decide and behave? Something like:

> *I want to ensure that my wife and daughter will always have a comfortable home; to earn enough money to take care of their needs and provide the best education possible for my daughter; and to be physically and emotionally present, kind, generous, open, and compassionate.*

Better. Much better. Why? Because now not only do I know what's important, what matters, but I also know how that information will guide my decisions and actions. Now, if I'm presented with an opportunity to invest my time or attention or money in something, I can ask:

> *Will this move me closer to ensuring a comfortable home for my wife and daughter, earning enough money to take care of their needs, and providing the best education possible for my daughter? Will it allow me to be more physically and emotionally present, kind, generous, open, and compassionate?*

If yes, I'm in. If no, I'm out. And if I'm weighing two options, I can choose the one that gets me closest. Expressed this way, a simple value now becomes an actionable value. It becomes useful in guiding my everyday decisions and actions. That's the place we want to get to with our top five values.

Now it's time to do the work yourself.

Daily Exploration:

Step 1—*Write down your basic values. Use the above list of values as a starting point, but don't be limited to them.*

If there's something that's not on the list but you feel it is really important, go with it. Start by just brainstorming all the possible things that are important to your life. Make your list as long as you like. Pure stream-of-consciousness. Do not do any editing yet.

Step 2—*Now, take a look at your list and circle the five values you feel most strongly about.*

Go with your gut. And just as a reminder, this is not about what you wish your answers were, or what you want others to think; it's about what they truly are.

Step 3—*Look at each of your top five values, and write them into a sentence that gives them context and definition.*

Be sure to include a verb. Spend a little time refining these sentences. Then, on a new piece of paper, write all five down.

Step 4—*Place that piece of paper somewhere you can see it or reference it whenever you want.*

As opportunities come your way throughout the day, ask yourself, "Does saying yes move me closer to what I hold most dear?" If the answer is no, whether it's checking your e-mail every 10 minutes or taking a new job, just say no. And start to say yes to only what genuinely matters most to you.

DAY 3

TAP your STRENGTHS

Statuesque in the moonlight, Julia drifted quietly from the group. Her bare feet waded through the grass, arriving at the edge of the fire. She knelt where she thought no one would see and began to weep.

I'd been watching the whole time, but I knew she needed room. To breathe. To be. After a few minutes, I made my way over and leaned in to give her a hug. She looked at me, trying to hold it together. Wanting with every cell in her body to be seen, but not judged as weak. Or selfish. Or incompetent.

Tears glimmered in the light of the flames. "She asked us to think of a time when we felt like we were at our best," Julia offered, "but it's been so long and I'm so spent, I couldn't even remember. I couldn't think of the last time I felt like I was *that* person." Tears returned. And my heart broke a little bit.

The "she" Julia was talking about was Emiliya Zhivotovskaya, whom we met in the earlier chapter on exercise and movement. A graduate of the master's program in applied positive psychology at the University of Pennsylvania, Zhivotovskaya is also on our Good Life Project faculty. She was with us in Costa Rica to introduce key ideas from the world of positive psychology. The thing that triggered such a strong reaction in Julia was something called character strengths. What are they? According to the "father" of positive psychology, Martin Seligman, character strengths "are most essential to who we are." They're not about your particular skills, gifts, or abilities. They go deeper. Character deep.

Rather than working entirely on the job of fixing what's wrong in our life, Seligman argues, if we understand our strengths, then build as much of our life as possible around them, much of what's wrong seems to fall away. We feel like we're tapping the most essential positive parts of ourselves to contribute to the world in a way that makes us feel immensely satisfied. We begin to become our strongest, most aligned, best selves. We come alive. There's now a mountain of research that backs up these claims.[22] Live from a place of embodied strengths and not only does your Contribution Bucket get fuller, your life gets better.

Zhivotovskaya, in fact, is a powerful example. Not just because she studies and now teaches strengths, but because she's lived both sides of the strengths equation. Fleeing religious persecution and the Chernobyl nuclear disaster as a child in Ukraine, she landed in the United States speaking only Russian. Shortly after, she witnessed her brother drown at the beach. Zhivotovskaya had every reason to be angry and withdrawn, and for a time, she was. Yet somehow she found a way to connect with the deeper parts of herself that represented her "true" self, her essential character. Where did that lead her? First to a dozen years as a party entertainer, leading thousands through nearly every Macarena and chicken-dance variation known to the planet. Zhivotovskaya embodied her best self when she helped others feel lifted and alive. That eventually led her to become a yoga teacher and coach, to pursue her master's degree in applied positive psychology and her Ph.D. in mind-body medicine. She is now building the largest certification program in positive psychology in the world.

Would it surprise you to learn that Zhivotovskaya's number one strength is zest, and love of learning is right up there next to it? Turns out Zhivotovskaya intuitively found a way to identify and tap her strengths to become a force of light in the world. Coming from a place of strength, she discovered another powerful truth: adversity is an invitation, not an end.

As Zhivotovskaya shared her story and the idea of embodying your strengths with Julia in Costa Rica years later, the wheels in Julia's brain began to turn. From the outside looking in, it would appear she had so many reasons to be grateful. A mom with a loving husband and healthy kids, she was building a career, had plenty of friends and interests, and put on a great show of health. She knew she was, in many ways, blessed. But that did little to soothe the undercurrent of yearning. Her deeper reality, as with so many of us, told a very different story.

She had been living from a place of stifled strengths and buried potential. Feeling like the "real" her, the strong, confident her, all the things that made her truly, radiantly, powerfully her, were screaming to get out, to reclaim their place as the center of her life. But she'd pushed them down, refused to live from that place for so long, she couldn't even remember the last time she felt like her best self. The self that embodied the most positive elements of her character. Her strengths-driven, lit-up self.

As she stood there with me in the night air on the side of a mountain overlooking the shimmering lights of Costa Rica's capital city, the facade was beginning to crack. She was beginning to own her inner desire to take back life's wheel and step into a profoundly different reality. To move through each day feeling like each ability, each strength, was being used to its fullest. To make the gap between her potential and her reality nonexistent. To live in the radiant glow of her best self.

Along with the tears and the yearning, gentle rays of hope meandered through the widening cracks in her splintering armor. And, for the first time in years, she began to see a path from pain and powerlessness to potential.

That, of course, leads to the big question.

How do you discover your strengths? Seligman and his colleague at the University of Michigan, Christopher Peterson, spent years researching this. They eventually developed a powerful strengths assessment called the VIA Survey of Character Strengths. It began as a research tool that asked a series of detailed questions, then kicked back a list that revealed how you ranked across 24 different strengths. The top five are, with rare exception, what they call your signature strengths. These are the ones you are meant to focus on. This self-assessment tool has been refined over the years, used in hundreds of academic studies and completed by more than 2.5 million people across more than 190 countries, amassing a stunning database of information.[23]

You may have heard of another strengths assessment, by the way, called the Clifton StrengthsFinder 2.0. That tool was based on the work of educational psychologist Donald Clifton and the Gallup Organization and also offers great insights. The focus is a bit different, though. It's less about core character traits and life in general and more about what they call your "dominant talents" and how you apply them in the world of work.

We actually use both tools in our work, because they give you different information. For our purposes and today's exploration, we're going to focus on the VIA strengths, because they're more broadly tailored to help you contribute meaningfully to all aspects of life, not just work. They are also extremely well researched, with many peer-reviewed, published studies substantiating their value. As a side benefit, as you're about to discover, the VIA Survey is also available for you to complete for free online. And that leads us to today's action step.

Daily Exploration:

Step 1—*Take the VIA Survey.*

Today you're going to set aside about 15 to 20 minutes to take your VIA Survey and discover your signature strengths (the top 5), along with your other character strengths (19 more). You can take the VIA Survey for free at viacharacter.org. Head on over when you have the time, then take the survey. And because we love accountability, once you've discovered your top five strengths, share them with your Good Life Project team and in our Good Life Project online community. You'll be able to see many others' strengths while you're there.

Step 2—*Integrate your strengths.*

Now that you've found your signature strengths, zoom the lens out a bit and ask yourself, "How can I build as many of these strengths into my day as possible?" For example, one of my top strengths is love of learning. I am my best self, loving life more and better equipped to contribute most meaningfully to the world, when I am immersed in the process of learning. I also know that I'm an autodidact, which is a fancy word for "total control freak who doesn't learn well in classrooms or any other setting where I don't control the information flow, setting, or pace." I've discovered that I learn best from books and programs where I can control the pace and focus only on what I find most interesting. I also learn well from individuals in private conversations, when I can ask exactly what I want to know. Building on this, I now wake up early and read every morning before anyone else rises. When I'm in a good rhythm, I'll end up reading a book or two a week and be in total heaven. That not only informs everything I create, but puts me in a really good place for the rest of the day. I feel like I am alive, like I can bring my best self to the world.

Take a few minutes after you've identified your strengths to look at the way you contribute to the world and also the way you move through your day. Think about how you might organically integrate more of your strengths into the things you already do, or shift the way you do them to allow you to bring more of your strengths to the work. Then explore whether there is something entirely new, like my morning reading routine, that you might create in your day to help you live from a place of embodied strength. Go ahead and write down at least three possible actions. Then begin to do them.

DAY 4

find your KILLER APP

Time to build on the Contribution triple threat: sparks, strengths, and values. Spark yourself, tap into your character strengths, and align your actions with what matters most to you, and you'll find your Contribution Bucket rapidly filling. If you were to do nothing else but focus on these three things, the way you contribute to the world would fill you up to a level you've likely never experienced. Still, we're just getting going!

Let's add something fun to your Contribution Bucket–filling toolbox, a little something I call your "killer app." What is that? Simple. It's the thing or things you're really good at. It's the unique blend of skill, talent, knowledge, and practice that has led to expertise and mastery. Put another way, it's the stuff you kick ass at and know like your mama knows your face. And before you think, "But I'm not really good at anything" or "I really don't know anything that well," stop. You are, and you do. We're all good, really good, at something, often many things. We often just don't see it or don't want to own it even if we do see it.

Maybe your killer app is needlepoint or quadratic equations. Maybe it's teaching or design. Maybe it's organizing crazy events or geeking out on spreadsheets. Maybe it's being a mom or dad or companion or caregiver, helping others find joy in the midst of adversity. Maybe it's a freakish knowledge of history or science or pop culture. Maybe it's just the calm, centered energy you're able to bring to the most frazzling of circumstances, a radiant ease that lets people exhale in your presence.

Some may call it a talent or gift, or maybe it's something we've put in years to master or get really good at. It's not about being the best, but about having achieved some level of proficiency. Nor do we really care where it comes from. We can leave the nature-versus-nurture debate for another time. We just need to know what it is, so that we can do more of it as we move through each day. Because when we do, we feel better. And we live better. The sense of purpose and engaged potential that comes when we work from a place of deep competence or mastery is near-intoxicating.

That said, I have to share a quick warning with you. Just because you can, doesn't mean you should. For the most part, the way you become really good at something or develop some level of expertise is to work really hard at it. That level of effort is most often fueled by something internal, your spark. But on occasion, and this happens more often when you're younger, you or those around you will notice you have a natural affinity for something. So they push you to do it more and more, until eventually you become great at it. If the early, external pushes lead to a level of proficiency that starts to light you up from within, that's awesome. But if the only reason you've become good at something is because someone else forced you to—and maybe continues to force it on you—then doing more of it may not, in fact, lead you to feel better. It may do the opposite. So beware the source of mastery when you think about integrating more of what you're good at into your life.

And that, of course, brings us to the big question.

What's your killer app?

For some of you, your killer app is on the tip of your tongue. If I asked, you'd immediately know it. For others, it might not be so apparent. And for still others, you may think you know, but there is something else lurking in the shadows that's your real killer app. Often it's something you won't acknowledge because doing so means acting on it, and while that can lead to bliss, it can also lead you to a pretty vulnerable place. If you've spent your life being warned away from ever being the tall poppy or shining light in the room, going public with your great big self may trigger feelings of unease. But at some point, you've got to get comfortable with a simple truth: the pride that rides in the saddle of extreme competence is not, by default, arrogance or hubris.

Standing tall in your abilities does not demand that you make others feel small. Instead, do it with grace, humility, and a fierce commitment to lift others along the way. If those others experience this as a source of envy or a threat, that's for them to resolve, not you. I know, easier said than done. Trust me; I've been on both sides. But I've also learned that when you bury your abilities in the name of avoiding judgment or attention, you do more harm than good. To yourself and your ability to live a good life and contribute at the level you're capable of, and to the world, which is denied the gift of your wisdom, presence, competence, and mastery.

When you contribute to the world in a way that taps your killer app, something kind of magical can happen. Competence becomes confidence. That feeling of radiant ease. Like you're doing something you're truly extraordinary at.

There's a certain grace that comes from leveraging mastery as a source of contribution. Interesting thing, too: the harder-won the skill, the better it feels. If your abilities come easily, you chalk it up mostly to genes or innate talent. You don't give yourself credit for having developed it and, in turn, don't derive as much satisfaction applying it. When you've worked fiercely to become good at something, sparked from within, you know what it's taken to get where you are, and that makes you appreciate what you're able to do so much more.

So, are you ready to figure out your killer app? We'll do that in today's exploration.

Daily Exploration:

It's time to figure out your killer app. There are a few different approaches to this, which I share below. Choose which feels most right for you.

Approach #1—*Look within.*
Some lucky folks immediately know their killer app or apps. They know they're amazing at spreadsheet modeling or painting or being a dad or listening or solving personal problems or match-making. If that's you, and as you read this chapter your killer app quickly popped into your mind, take a few minutes and write it down now. If there's more than one, that's fine. Some of us are deeply knowledgeable or really good at one big thing. Others have more of a blend.

Approach #2—*Look to others.*
I've had a pretty solid sense of my killer apps for many years. One is an ability to see possibility, especially in others, and cre-ate experiences—books, businesses, communities, brands, events, and more—that move them to see and embrace it. Still, I'm always curious about what I'm not seeing. As my friend Charlie Gilkey likes to tell me, "You can't read the label from inside the jar." So a few years back, I decided to ask a group of people two questions:

1. What do you come to me for, or where do you see me offering substantial value?

2. What do you thank me for?

That second question came from another friend, Danielle LaPorte, author of the book *The Desire Map: A Guide to Creating Goals with Soul.*[24]
It was fascinating to see how people answered these questions. Many of the answers were exactly what I thought they'd be. Oth-ers took me by surprise and led me down paths I never would have considered. One pattern that emerged when I asked the question caused me to make changes to the way I serve others and earn

my living. A consistent response to the second question—What do you thank me for?—was about not what I "did," but who I "was." We don't thank you so much for what you tell us, came the answers, but more for the energy you bring to a room or experience. It took me a while to figure out how to leverage that in building my career. In fact, I fought it and continue to fight it on some level—in part because my business brain says, "Well, you can't scale intimate presence," and in part because it still weirds me out to think that I or anyone can matter simply because we're there. Still, knowing this had led me to make choices that honor what I've learned. The more I own it, the easier things get.

So, what about you? Take a few minutes to make a list of 20 to 50 people who you feel know you well. It's nice to draw upon a cross-section from your work, personal, social, and family life, if you can. Then head over to goodlifeproject.com/bookinsider. I've created a model e-mail that you can copy and paste and tweak to make it more personal. Do that, then take a deep breath and hit send. When you start to get replies, look less for the details and more for the big patterns. They'll help guide you. And, especially, look for surprises. They may lead you to explore integrating things you never thought of into more of your life.

Approach #3—*Take a scientific approach: StrengthsFinder 2.0.*
Remember when I discussed character strengths in the prior chapter, I mentioned there are two major schools of thought? One is the VIA Survey, which identifies character strengths (you now know your top five). You can think of them almost like your most positive character traits or virtues. The other is the Clifton StrengthsFinder 2.0 assessment mentioned in the prior chapter. The reason we often tap both in the work we do at Good Life Project is that they tell us different things. StrengthsFinder 2.0 is less about character and more about identifying specific talents, knowledge, and skills. In other words, it's about helping you find your killer app, so you can do more of it. The great thing about StrengthsFinder 2.0 is that, similar to the VIA Survey, there are now data based on the millions of people who've taken the assessment to validate it. So if you want a complimentary scientifically

validated approach to add to the mix of intuition and inquiry, you should consider taking this assessment. You can also find it directly at strengths.gallup.com.

Regardless of the approach you take, the final bit of homework for today is this: Do the work to identify your killer app. Then write down three to five ways you might be able to integrate more of it into the way you contribute to the world.

DAY 5

GET OUT OF YOUR HEAD

A few years back, when I was in the fitness world, I came up with an idea for a revolutionary "ropeless" jump rope. This thing would have been world changing. It would have opened a wonderful, accessible form of exercise to millions who felt like they just didn't have the coordination for an old-school rope. I thought through all the details, all the arguments, pros and cons. Then, as often happens, I got busy. And admittedly, I have a bit of entrepreneurial ADD (understatement of the century).

So I tucked it away, until one fateful night, while watching TV, I was jarred to a stop by an infomercial. Those #*$&#s stole my idea!!!

How many times has that happened to you? You get a flash of genius. Who knows where it comes from; you're just glad it happened. An idea drops seemingly from the sky. Maybe it's a juicy recipe or an invention or a book or a business. Oh my, this is going to be big! Then you start to think about it. And think about it. And think about it.

Pretty soon, you realize multiple parties, warring factions simultaneously having two or three sides of a conversation, have inhabited your head. The debate in your noggin rages on. This is stupid, argues one side. No, it's genius, argues the other. Do it this way, argues one side. What, are you kidding me? counters the other; that's idea suicide. Questions and scenarios spin around at a blinding pace as you think things through, trying to figure out what's legit and what's destructive self-talk. Without even realizing it, weeks or even months pass. You've thought the idea through mercilessly, but still, it's locked tight in the space between your ears. You may even think you've come to a "logical" conclusion and kill it, but in fact, if you've never done anything to take the idea from your head into the world, there's a good chance the decision is more about fear than logic.

Here's the thing about ideas. They're worthless. Okay, so maybe they're not worthless, but they don't matter unless and until you do something with them. Millions of people have seemingly amazing ideas all day, every day. It's not the idea that has value; it's what happens to it when it interacts with the world. And what happens to you. Picasso said it beautifully: "To know what you're going to draw, you have to begin drawing." Get out of your head. Draw. Play. Move. Love. Hug. Ask. Write. Speak. Test. Make. Build.

The greatest stories ever told weren't great because they were thought. They were great because they were expressed.

And with rare exception, they weren't great the first time offered. Or the second, tenth, or one-hundredth. Ideas need to be worked. That starts in your head, but at some point the process needs to move into the world. When that happens, everything changes. Instead of responding to self-talk and fear and a million permutations of "what if," you end up responding to information. You get actual rather than imagined feedback. You discover whether your crazy idea will work and, if not, what you'd need to do to make it work. You cannot *think* your way to an outcome. You've got to *act* your way to it.

Why don't we act, then?

Why don't we immediately go from "what if" to "let me try it out, see how I feel about it and, if it matters, how others respond to it"? Why are we so locked into spinning tales in our heads rather than stories in the world? Simple answer. Fear. We fear being judged for having a crazy idea, going for it, and failing. Nobody can judge you for an idea they never knew existed. When you share an idea, it becomes real. So does the possibility of failure and judgment. We'd do pretty much anything to avoid that, including destroying the opportunity for success.

Researcher and best-selling author of *Daring Greatly* and *Rising Strong*, Brené Brown has studied this phenomenon extensively. Focusing on shame and vulnerability, she looks at how we stifle ourselves in order to avoid being vulnerable to rejection. As we sat together, "crisscross, applesauce" on my mom's couches one afternoon, she offered this:

> It is so easy to make a life and a career out of sitting in the bleachers. . . . There are people who have amazing gifts, who could make the world an incredibly better place, who won't put their work out there for [fear of judgment]. And that's a loss. And whether we know what that work was or not, we miss it and grieve it every day.
>
> There are songs that we need to hear, there are stories that need to be told, that we'll never see or know because there are so many people out there who are so reflectively cynical and critical and mean-spirited. I don't like it.

When you put your songs and stories into the world, you may be judged. They may not fly. But what if they do? Are you okay with destroying that possibility just because you're afraid?

Here's my invitation.

Step out of your head and into the world. Trust that what you're thinking about just might work. And even if it doesn't, the challenge of moving through an idea the world doesn't embrace almost always pales in comparison with the regret of never having offered it in the first place.

Daily Exploration:

Nietzsche said, "There is one path in the world that none can walk but you. Where does it lead? Don't ask, walk!" Time for the first step. Think about something you've been mulling over in your head. Something you'd love to see happen. Something that would matter, both to you and to those who might experience it. Write it down. Get specific. Then ask yourself, "Is there some piece of it I'd be okay sharing?" Even if it's just with one person, in the name of taking the first step. If you're struggling to find a person or group you feel comfortable with, think about jumping into our private online group, where you'll find all sorts of other folks in just the same place as you. You don't have to go 100-percent public with your bad self. Start with one-percent public with your moderately bad self.

DAY 6

WOOP it UP

In my twenties, I took very little on faith. I always had to know the reason why. Show me the data, the science, the system or methodology. In my thirties, I began to experience things that would soften my lens, things both good and bad. Still, if there were data, I yearned to find the why behind the what. I spent a chunk of my late 30s and early 40s studying and teaching yoga and meditation and going deep into a science of another kind. Not just gross anatomy, but what the more energetically inclined would call the subtle body.

Words like *prana, ki, life-force, chakras, nadis, meridians, doshas,* and *akashic field* entered my realm. Though, truth be told, so much of my willingness to embrace them still hung on my ability to simultaneously overlay them with my knowledge of Western science, anatomy, and physiology. Talk to me about prana and I'd secretly think electromagnetic field. Talk about chakras and my practical brain would overlay the neural plexus. Talk about meridians and I'd see highly conductive fascial tissue. Still, I was becoming less demanding and more accepting when the easy analogy didn't come.

In my 40s, and heading into my 50s now, having embraced the wonder of fatherhood, the blessing of a deepening marriage, and the early edges of tragedy and suffering, grace and awe, I'm what I'd call open and practical. If there is no science but a phenomenon is real, I'm okay with the notion that something beyond my grasp is in control.

This actually happened in a funny way after I spoke on stage recently. A woman who'd been in the audience waited behind and, after everyone left, came very hesitantly to share something. "I'm not the aura lady," she said. "I don't go around seeing people's auras, but yours was so big for the first 15 minutes, I couldn't hear what you were saying. And it had a tail like a comet that was following you around the stage."

"Okay," I said, "that's cool." And, now, of course, I had to know. "What color was it?"

"Violet," she told me, and off she went.

Later that day, I met a friend in a coffee shop and recounted the story, without revealing the color. She looked at me and shared, "Yeah, I saw it, too."

"Oh, sure you did," I said. "What color?"

"Violet."

A few months later, I bumped into a friend and his girlfriend at a small gathering and repeated the story, again without revealing the color. The girlfriend was what I'd call decidedly woo-woo. She said she saw it, too, as I stood before her. Clear as day, it was violet.

Now, of course, the aura gauntlet had been thrice thrown down, so I had to know what violet meant. I took to the Internet. On allaurasandchakras.com, I learned that violets are unorthodox, inventive, intelligent, highly intuitive, visionary, big-picture thinkers with a profound yearning to make a difference and a relentless need for meaning. They're great at breakthrough ideas, seeing how things fit together in a way nobody else sees. But they're less interested in granular process, systems, and details. They have an uncanny ability to predict trends and see possibility, often long before it manifests, which can also lead to the frustrations of being perpetually "too early" to the market. They're passionate and emotional and experience life as a constant state of evolution and growth. Violets are spiritual, but often in a more universal and less faith-driven way. They need a lot of space for solitude and can often appear aloof or antisocial, though in reality they love people on a more selective level and revel in fewer, deeper conversations. "Out of power" violets can also be arrogant, thinking they can do everything better than anyone else, and so they try, leading them to feel overwhelmed, frustrated, and fatigued. They crash hard when they ignore their inner sense of mission or try to pursue many things at once, rather than going deep into a few.

The full description was far more extensive. I've taken nearly every personality assessment ever made, and the accuracy of the description made my jaw drop. So color me open to auras and other, not-so-easy-to-validate phenomena.

At the same time, if there is science out there, I want to know what it is. And if the science is strong and conflicts with the metaphysical or nonscientific explanation, you can be pretty sure I'm going to take the side of science. That's where I find myself with the whole notion of manifesting. Especially in the context of the laws and rules most often offered.

The idea has been around probably as long as we have. Want something to have or hold or happen? Think it into being. Want someone to drop into your life? Dream it into being. Specifics tend to vary a bit among leading books, movies, and teachers in the space, but the general process is:

1. Get crystal clear on what you want.

2. Create a detailed, tangible representation of it.

3. Ask the universe to deliver your vision into reality, to manifest it.

4. Do not try to figure out how to make it happen; simply hold yourself open for the answers and the outcomes to manifest themselves in your life.

5. Never ever, ever, ever think or ask questions about failure or obstacles or negative stuff, even if it's just trying to figure out why it happened in the past or how you might deal with it if it happens again, because that'll attract this negative stuff into your orbit.

As I mentioned, there are many variations. Proponents will argue that the subtleties matter, and that the reason one approach might work and another might not is about the little things.

I'm open to the idea that sometimes your best answers and opportunities come from hard work followed by space and surrender. I'm also good with the possibility that when you get very clear on what you want to create, your brain has what Harvard Medical School professor and neuropsychiatrist Srinivasan Pillay calls a hidden GPS system that sets in motion all manner of less-than-conscious processes needed to reveal the steps to make it happen.

But what I don't understand is the need for mystical explanations for why a process of manifestation might work, when there's actual hard science about what's happening. Nor do I buy the proclamation that even thinking about the possibility of obstacles and failure, or planning for them, makes you less likely to get what you want. The research, in fact, has been done, and the answer is clear. The exact opposite is true.

Maybe now you're starting to see why I have a bit of a love-hate relationship with the whole self-help version of manifesting. The word, alone, had a pretty great history until a few years back. At its root, it's really just about making things real. Taking something that exists in the ether of ideas or energy and turning it into something you can touch, feel, see, hear, or in some other way experience. Something horrible and feared can manifest as easily as something wonderful and desired. A hidden illness can manifest in symptoms. An idea can manifest as a book or business.

But in truth, manifesting is just a more passive version of goal achievement. And there's a ton of research on what it takes to turn dreams into realities. In. Real. Life.

Turns out that true manifestation doesn't come from a clear vision, a deep desire, blind faith, and a refusal to go to the dark side. It's not about seeing and wanting and willfully pushing away negative thoughts. In fact, research shows that those negatives have value. They just might be the missing pieces in the manifestation puzzle.

Enter Gabriele Oettingen, a professor of psychology at New York University and the University of Hamburg. She studies motivation and goal achievement, among other things, diving into how we maddeningly irrational humans think about and create our futures. In other words, she researches manifesting to figure out what actually works and what's total bunk. Oettingen is also the author of *Rethinking Positive Thinking: Inside the New Science of Motivation*, where she shares an interesting take on wishful delusion versus practical goal attainment.

In her lab, she found something pretty interesting. People who only *fantasized* about finding a new partner, getting a new job, recovering from surgery, or acing an exam fared much worse than those who fantasized and then took a few extra steps. The big winners were people who moved beyond fantasizing, acknowledged the major obstacles that were likely to appear, and planned how they'd handle them if and when they did appear.

Turns out acknowledging the very real likelihood of bad stuff happening along the way doesn't make you more likely to fail. It doesn't "repel" your dream outcome. Nor does supplementing your brain's GPS by actively pursuing solutions instead of waiting for them to be given from beyond. In fact, these things do the exact opposite. They make you acknowledge, quantify, and then choose whether you are willing to own what it will truthfully take to make your dream a reality. The potential suffering, the sacrifice, the stumbles and failures, and the judgment. They force you to examine the cost of the quest and then decide three things: What are the biggest potential obstacles? Do I still want it enough to endure those associated costs? And if so, how will I prepare in advance to deal with the challenges and costs if and when they come?

Oettingen has distilled her peer-reviewed, published research on wish attainment, or manifesting, into a simple and practical four-step method, easily remembered by the acronym WOOP.[25]

1. W—Wish. Identify something you want to have happen or something you want to accomplish. It should be something you really want, something that excites you, but also, deep down, something you believe is attainable.

2. O—Outcome. Describe the outcome that would unfold in your life upon attaining your wish. Make it emotional. Describe how it would make you feel, why it matters.

3. O—Obstacle. Think about the potential personal obstacles that will likely, or at least possibly, come up along the way. This often starts on an internal level, around fear or willpower or loss of confidence.

4. P—Plan. Detail what you'd do to overcome each obstacle, should it arise. Think, "If X happens, I will do Y."

The method is simple, and having now been thoroughly vetted, both in the lab and in practical application, it's been proven to work.

Does that mean I'm forever closed to other approaches? Of course not. But since there is proven science, I want to be convinced with science, not anecdotal data. At least to my knowledge, that hasn't happened yet with manifestation. Since I'm the practical yet open guy and I promised you a practical guide, at least for now I'm going to suggest we all spend a little more time WOOPing and a little less time waiting and hoping and ignoring. That brings us to today's exploration, your first WOOP.

Daily Exploration:

Let's try a little WOOPing, shall we? A bit of advice before diving in: You may be inclined to go big out of the gate. That's probably not a great idea. Pick something simple in the beginning. Something like "I want to walk for five minutes every morning before work." Two ways to go about it:

1. Use the WOOP My Life app. Because Oettingen isn't only about what happens in the lab, but also about what happens in life, she's turned the entire WOOP method into a free app that you can download. You can find it over at woopmylife.org. Spend a little time, think about something you'd like to make happen, then head on over and let the app be your guide.

2. Do it on paper. Over at goodlifeproject.com/bookinsider, I've included a full-page template designed to walk you through the process of creating your first manifestation quest using the WOOP method.

DAY 7

GIVE TO glow

A few years ago I was having one of those brutal days. Too much to do, lines everywhere, and patience nonexistent. My local post office in Hell's Kitchen, New York, was no exception. Twenty minutes in, and it was finally my turn. Package deposited, I fell into my New York stride. Do not look up. Do not acknowledge other living beings. And never, ever look another person in the eye. Just keep your head down and power through the bustling herd.

Moving to the post office steps, I made a fatal error. I glanced up. Standing before me was a young boy, maybe nine or ten years old. He was dressed in a blazer and tie with a school insignia. I was moving so fast, I almost knocked him over. But his kind gaze and innocent smile stopped me. He stood, anxiously looking up. "Excuse me, sir," he said, "would you like to buy a chocolate bar to support my school?"

A hit of compassion began to well inside me, but old habits die hard. For years, I'd come to see most anyone who asked for money on the street in the same vein. Pests, addicts, and thieves. Yes, even the kids. Plants used by parents to solicit money for drugs or alcohol. A decade earlier, on a different street in a different part of the city, as I rolled out of my then girlfriend's apartment early one weekend, a kind-looking couple approached, told me a story, and asked for money, which I gladly gave. Though I wouldn't discover the fact until later that day, I'd been conned. Sucker, said my friends. That's what happens when you trust people and act from a place of kindness. I felt like an idiot. A mark. Never again.

Yet there I stood, on the steps of the post office, some 10 years deeper into life, now a father and husband yearning to cultivate a gentler view. Before me this young boy was inviting me to reconsider my take on the issue. To be kind. To contribute to his world, without expectation.

My autopilot resolve ceded to a more compassionate inner voice. Less "Why are you bothering me?" and more "Who am I to judge?" I paused. He smiled insecurely. Pleadingly. I felt his unease. He didn't want to be asking any more than I wanted to be asked. I saw myself in his shoes, nervous and in need, and decided to accept the invitation. I offered a dollar for a bar and a thank-you. Chocolate in hand, I turned and began to make my way through the big glass doors, out onto the platform atop the final set of steps down to the street.

Glancing down toward the sidewalk, I caught a glimpse of an older gentleman, silver hair and glasses, leaning with some effort on a cane. As I made my way down the steps, his eyes locked onto mine and a gentle smile began to widen across his face. His eyebrows lifted, glasses slid down a bit on his nose. I couldn't resist smiling back. His smile widened to a grin. He was beaming as he began to raise his free hand ever so gently, leaning deeper into his cane with the other. I turned to see he was pointing at the young man inside on the steps.

"That's my grandson," he shared with some effort. Then, after a pause, "Thank you."

I was in tears. The rest of my day became magical.

There's actually a name for this feeling. It's called the "giver's glow." Stony Brook University School of Medicine professor Stephen Post reveals the science behind the experience in his book *Why Good Things Happen to Good People: How to Live a Longer, Healthier, Happier Life by the Simple Act of Giving*.[26] Turns out even the mere thought of being of service to others activates the part of the brain that releases the feel-good neurotransmitter dopamine. That makes us feel great and want to do more. It triggers an enhanced sense of purpose and well-being and gives us that deeply yearned-for feeling that we matter. That the things we do, at least in the moment, have meaning.

Giving, it turns out, not only begets more giving, feeling good, and wanting to do more, but also deepens our sense of purpose. It fills our Contribution and Vitality Buckets and, depending on who is on the other end of our generosity, might also fill our Connection Bucket, too. But not all giving is equal, and not all givers win. Adam Grant, beloved professor from the Wharton School at the University of Pennsylvania who is mentioned again later in this book, has spent years studying the act of giving. In his book *Give and Take: A Revolutionary Approach to Success*, he shares some eye-opening research.[27] Givers, he offers, generally end up on the extreme ends of life's success spectrum. They're heavily represented among the big winners, the people with great lives, and also among the big losers, those who've crashed and burned. Pardon the pun, but what gives?

The answer, according to Grant comes down to "who we help, how we help, and when we help." We'd love to think that those who just give everything they have to anyone who asks, the most generous, selfless people, are the ones who win big. Sadly, the opposite is true. Those who give indiscriminately more often end up on the losing end of life. When you really think about this, it makes sense. If you spend every day satisfying everyone else's needs, you have nothing left for your own needs, your own visions, goals, quests, desires, hopes, and aspirations. As Grant shared in a recent conversation with *On Being*'s Krista Tippett:

> Failed givers are the people who help anyone. . . . One of the mistakes failed givers make is that they drop anything for every request that comes in. You see with successful givers, they're much more likely to prioritize and say, 'Okay, I've got these windows blocked to make sure I can progress on my own tasks, and then I have other

periods of time set aside to try to be helpful and responsive to others.' . . . If there's not [any balance], you're at much higher risk for burnout and you're at much higher risk for being exploited. It's just like on an airplane, you have to secure your oxygen mask before assisting others. . . .

The irony is, if you look at 30-plus years of data on this, the people who are the most selfless, the most altruistic, actually give less than the people who balance concern for others with concern for self. . . . If you are selfless to the point of self-sacrifice, at some point you run out of energy and resources to be able to contribute to others. Whereas people who are able to work toward their own goals, or at least keep their own interests in their rearview mirror when they're helping others, are able to sustain their energy and their resources, and that allows them to give much more over time.

When we think about giving, we often think about grand gestures, setting aside hours or days to volunteer, mentor, or contribute to some person or group we want to see rise. Or we think about specific charities, foundations, and organizations to donate to. But giving even on the smallest level has power. So often, we miss the momentary opportunities to contribute, the countless moments to be generous, to help, to be of service in the moment, for a moment. That's the beauty of the chocolate bar story. Nothing was planned, it happened in the blink of an eye, but everything was changed and, years, later, I still feel it when I share the story.

There is another surprising aspect to giving. I never really keyed in on it until Grant turned me on to a study done by positive psychology professor Sonja Lyubomirsky. She had a group do one act of kindness a day, five days a week for 10 weeks. A second group did five acts of kindness all on the same day of the week, also for 10 weeks. Grant calls this "sprinkling" (one a day) versus "chunking" (five a day). Intuitively, you'd probably think the sprinkle approach would make you happier. You get a little sprinkle of giver's glow every day. Lyubomirsky found the exact opposite. Only the chunkers experienced any meaningful mood boost from their generosity. Why? Nobody really knows, but the effect was clear. It argues for focused and intentional giving within one specific window on a regular basis. For example, turn every Friday into Give Five Day. Or, if you're inclined, I've got another really fun way to experiment with this in today's daily exploration.

Daily Exploration:

Today's exploration is called the Give30. My experience with the grandpa, the kid, and the chocolate bar made me smile for a day. Then, like so many other wonderful opportunities, it ended up buried as a lovely memory. But it never left me. Every once in a while, I'd wonder what might happen if, instead of waiting for opportunities to give, I actively looked for them for an entire day. This was before I had even heard about sprinklers and chunkers. I gave it a try and began to notice that every time I looked, I'd find opportunities with ease. They weren't the rare treasures I thought them to be, waiting to drop into my life by chance. They were all around me, hiding in plain view. All I needed to do was see them.

Sometimes these moments involved giving a little bit of money, but far more often they were simply about giving a moment of my time, my patience, my love, myself. I'd flag a cab for a stranger in need on the corner. I'd spend a few minutes helping a friend figure out a tough conversation. I'd help my daughter or wife, mother or father, figure something out. I'd hold a door (though that's gotten me into trouble, too; what some consider manners, others consider sexism). I'd mentor a student or entrepreneur. I'd teach or speak or donate money. I'd make a quick introduction by e-mail or phone. I'd take an extra beat to notice the name of the barista making my morning coffee and thank them personally for taking such good care of me. You may think so many of these things are just common courtesy, but in a world where speed and distraction trump presence and generosity, sadly they've become the exception rather than the rule.

I decided to take things to the next level and run an experiment. For one day, every time I had an opportunity to give, to offer an act of kindness that would take me less than 30 seconds or cost me less than a dollar, I had to do it, up to 30 times that day. My maximum investment in time and money would be a total of 15 minutes and/or 15 dollars. As I carried out my plan, I noticed that the opportunities almost always arose in a window between other activities, so it really didn't take me away from other important things. And the money never approached the 15-dollar cap. I called it my Give30 experiment. I didn't tell anyone I was doing it, not even my wife.

Two things happened. One, simply knowing it was a Give30 day shifted my mindset. It put me in a state of heightened awareness and anticipation, always scanning for opportunities to help. That subtle shift, alone, made me feel amazing. I was walking through each day looking for chances to be generous. Then there was the giver's glow from the nearly 30 smiles, thanks, and hugs. I also realized it actually wasn't about being thanked or recognized. Even when gratitude didn't come, simply knowing that in some small way I'd helped was all I needed. Total investment: 15 minutes and rarely more than a few dollars. Total impact on both my Contribution and Vitality Buckets: priceless. Now it's your turn.

Make today your first Give30 day. You don't have to plan anything. If money is a challenge, focus more on helping in some other way. You don't have to do big, public acts. You just have to move through the day open to the many opportunities to help that, on most other days, you remain blind to. Simple, often momentary acts of service, kindness, or generosity. At the end of the day, write in your journal about the experience and how it made you feel. If you're inclined, share your experience with your Good Life Project teammates.

DAY 8

PRACTICE The Loving NO

I'm coming into town next week; can we grab a bite together? Maybe go for a walk? Now that I think about it, do you mind if I crash on your couch for a few weeks? Can you pick me up from the airport? At rush hour? After I get my luggage? At that little airport three hours away because, you know, it's cheaper to fly into?

Can you do me a quick fave, too, and grab some stuff from the market for me? I'll text you the list. Plus, I was thinking it would be soooo great if you'd help out on the fund-raiser this year, and could you maybe even organize the talent for next month's block party?

That's all cool with you, right? Right?

Ah, life. With seemingly millions of people wanting a piece of you. It's awesome, flattering, and lovely to be loved and wanted. Admired. Valued. Treasured. How many others would like to be in your position? How blessed is your life? Seriously, you're not going to complain about being needed, right?

Short answer: no. You're not going to complain. It's awesome. It is a true blessing. But you *are* going to do something about it. Because, without intervention, what I've just described has the potential to become not life lived well, but death by a thousand asks.

Knowing what you want out of life, and who you want in it, means nothing if you can't also say no to everything but those people and things. Until you cultivate the ability to say no to the things that fill your life but not your soul, you'll never have the space to bring into it the things you desperately want to say yes to.

Think about it this way. Life is a jigsaw puzzle, and you're building this puppy on the kitchen table. Each piece has one of two words written on it, *yes* or *no*. There's a mix of both, and all the pieces of your puzzle are filled in. This is a weird puzzle, though. The box comes with a bunch of extra pieces, ones that say both *yes* and *no*. Stepping back from the table, you think you're done but then realize you're not digging the way it looks. Something's not quite right. You figure it out. It would look so much better with one more yes piece, and you've found the perfect piece. But there's no place to put it. The puzzle is completely filled in. You can't add a yes until you've gotten rid of a no.

That puzzle is your life, with one difference. In life, we don't want to accept the fact that the size of the puzzle is the size of the puzzle. We keep trying to expand it, to turn a 50-piece puzzle into 100 pieces. The bigger it gets, we figure, the better the puzzle. There are ways to do that, within limits. Work longer. Ten more pieces. Get more efficient. Add 10 pieces. Use technology. Add 10 more. Delegate. Oh, that'll get you 20.

At some point, though, the puzzle gets so big that it starts to hit the edge of the table. That's life's true capacity. You can't add more pieces without the edges falling off the table. Without random pieces of your life tumbling onto the old linoleum floor. At a certain point, the answer is not efficiency; it's subtraction. The only way to add a new piece, one you desperately want because it'll make the whole thing so much better, is to get rid of a different one first.

How do we do that in life? Start saying no.

Start pulling out the pieces you no longer want and saying no to the ones everyone else wants you to put back in.

Okay, but how do you know what to say no to? It all seems so good. Can't you just do and have it all? Plus, it's so nice to be wanted. If you start saying no, people might not want you anymore, right?

Let's talk about that last bit first, because it's a huge myth. As long as you keep doing what made people want you, being less available won't make them want you less. It will make them want you more. Even if they have to wait. A long time.

Fun example: Wayne Henderson makes guitars. Working out of a small shop in the hills of Virginia, he's one of the best. But there's only one of him—and a lot of people who want guitars from him. He doesn't care. He works the way he works, doing what he wants at the speed that feels right. When guitar legend Eric Clapton came looking for a Wayne Henderson guitar, he did what everyone else does. He waited. Ten years.

If the magic that draws others to want it from you is so fleeting or illusory that making it harder to get quickly renders it obsolete, then you don't have something worth worrying about.

But there's a bigger point. How do you know what to say no to? For that one, you'll want to refer back to the "Know What Matters" chapter, where I share a pretty straightforward way to make that call. I'm guessing there's still an unanswered question on your mind. Exactly how do you say no in a way that doesn't crush people's spirits, make everyone hate you, or make you feel like you've just ruined their lives— or at least the thing they wanted you to help with?

A mentee, Sandy, recently came to me and said:

> I always get e-mails from people who want to meet up when they come to town. Or they want me to look something over for them. I just got one, and it's from someone I don't really know, but she feels like she knows me. She's coming to town and wants to grab dinner. I know I don't have the time, I know exactly what I'd rather and should

be doing, but I feel terrible saying no. What if she hates me for it?

Two thoughts. One, there are direct and kind ways to phrase things. While they don't take the entire sting out, they soften the blow enough for you to feel you've done the right thing in the right way. Ask yourself, "How can I be kind and respectful yet also stand strong in what I need? What would that sound like?" Everyone's words will be different. Two, what if that other person does hate you for it? If it's someone not central to your life, it's probably a good thing you learned how they respond to boundaries before they became central. And if it is someone central, then maybe it's a great time to begin the process of defining better boundaries for both you and that person.

I get requests like this a lot. They come via e-mail, Facebook, Twitter, Instagram, and even good old snail mail. It's great to feel valued, and I'd love to be able to make everyone happy. But at the same time, I need a pretty big chunk of time to make real progress in the work that is most meaningful to me, and to honor my commitment to be present with my family and do the things needed to fill my Vitality Bucket. Much as it pains me to say no, I have to. And so do you. Because if we don't, everything suffers. The work we hold most sacred and the relationships we hold most dear end up taking a back seat to the list of obligations we've felt bound to say yes to. We have to own the fact that we're human, there's only one of us, and sadly, that means most requests for time, energy, and attention that lie outside the things that most effectively fill our Good Life Buckets need to be answered with a kind no. It's the kind that creates space for the hell yes.

Now it's time for you to start practicing the art of the loving but firm no.

Daily Exploration:

Let's start simple. Think about a request that's currently being made of you to which the answer should be no, but you just can't get up the gumption to let fly the loving no. Ask what saying yes would stop you from doing that matters so much more. Same question if you're already doing something you want to dump and this is about saying no to continuing. Picture yourself spending all the time you've now freed up doing the thing that matters more. Now grab your pen or open your computer. (If you're going to write an e-mail, please remember this: never, ever, *ever* put the recipient's e-mail address in the "to" field until you are 100 percent done crafting the body of your message.) Then start writing.

A few tips:

1. *Keep it short and be direct.* Yes, I know you're going to feel the need to gush rhapsodic about how wonderful the person is and how fabulous the opportunity is and how you've loved the way they dressed since third grade and you hope they don't hate you for it and did they know how tough life has been lately and how many crazy things have been happening, so let me list them. Every. Single. One. Some of which are true. But don't. That's about you, not them. They already know, love, and respect you or they don't. Buttering them up, creating extravagant emotional buffering schemes and bunkers to hide in before delivering the no is disempowering and leaves both of you feeling icky.

2. *Begin with gratitude, both in your heart and on the page.* No matter how swamped you are, the fact that someone wants something from you is pretty darn awesome. It's a good thing. Honor that, taking a brief moment to switch from "Oy, this person is so annoying" to "How awesome. I'm thankful." Then thank them for their kind invitation or offer and say you're grateful they considered you for it.

3. *Say no, and share a single, understandable, and incontrovertible reason why.* Rather than offer a laundry list of reasons, thinking the more you pile on, the

more they'll believe you, pick a single reason that is most powerful and state it without apology.

4. *Offer an alternative solution.* If you know another person who might help, offer to make the connection or simply refer them.

5. *Wish them success.* Because you really do want them to get what they need, just not from you on the terms they're demanding.

6. *Thank them again.* Simple enough.

DAY 9

LOVE the JOB you're WITH

In the 1988 movie *Coming to America*, Eddie Murphy's character, a wealthy royal named Prince Akeem, sets out in search of a wife who'll love him for who he is, not what he has. He heads to New York City and, hiding his regal lineage, takes a job mopping and cleaning at a fast-food place. Now, I enjoy a schmaltzy love story as much as the next person, but the thing that always stayed with me about this movie was how joyful, grateful, and proud his character appeared to be while doing a job that so many others might view as soul sucking, stressful, low-paying, or even beneath them. I wondered, "Is that really possible outside the movies?"

I've worked my share of similar jobs, from washing dishes to lugging railroad ties and sorting sweepstakes lottery entries. It really doesn't matter what the job is or even how it pays. You could be a neurosurgeon but still experience it as an utterly gutting pursuit. One person's contribution hell is another's heaven. It's completely subjective. The only truth when you're doing life-sucking work is that it's sucking *your* life.

Then why not just leave? That's certainly one option, especially if you're young and there's not much on the line yet. Go find another gig. Life's too short; do what you love. That's certainly the rallying cry we hear from a good bit of the self-help world. If you choose that path, the things you'll discover about yourself in this book will help you choose a path that is more aligned with who you are and what really matters to you. But it's not the entire story. The further you get into life, the harder that advice is to take. Leaving anything, even something you hate, will cause a certain amount of pain and disruption, both for you and for anyone else who counts on you. The more you've built around the money and security of your current career, illusory as both may be, the more the pain of blowing it up. Few people are willing to endure that, no matter how much the pain of staying eats at their soul. So they just sit tight and suffer.

There's also another truth, and maybe this is yours. For millions, it's just not possible or appropriate to leave, even if your job is brutally hard and pays you nothing. If your primary job is taking care of your kids through a challenging time or an aging parent who is deeply abusive but without means, chances are you're not looking for easier kids or a less abusive, richer parent to swap out. It is what it is. Still, there is hope.

What if there was a way to take something that, on the surface, might seem to add little beyond money (if that) to your Contribution Bucket, or might even seem to deplete it, and turn it into a bucket-filling faucet-of-love? What if there was a way to avoid the pain of leaving a job (or honor the fact that you can't) and make staying more bearable or, potentially, even deeply rewarding and meaningful? What if there was a way to teach yourself to love the job you're with? Not because *it* has changed, but because *you* have.

In *Man's Search for Meaning*, neurologist and psychiatrist, Viktor Frankl, offered an unnerving and provocative invitation.[28] Frankl endured the death of his family and the worst atrocities and conditions imaginable in the Holocaust camps of World War II. He was also forced into service as a physician, which became, in part, his salvation. From this place, this "situation," he was able to survive by finding a greater purpose in his role and intense meaning through immutable suffering. "When we are no longer able to change the situation," Frankl wrote, "we are challenged to change ourselves." That's our starting point. The idea that something beyond pure circumstance determines our experience of work and life. The possibility that we might derive profound meaning from our work not by changing the work, but by changing the way we look at it.

Over the years, I'd many times heard stories of nuns who went about what would be considered the most menial and repetitive of tasks, basic cleaning and service, in the exact same way, every day for decades. Others might have experienced this same job with deep resentment and futility, yet the nuns found it to be a source of devotion and communion, profound connection and contribution to the Divine and to their sacred community. Monotony transformed to meaning. I'd also read about monks who would rise early every morning and spend hours slowly and meticulously sweeping and cleaning the meditation room before others arrived, experiencing it as a form of deep service and meditation. This made sense because it happened in a setting steeped in service, stillness, and devotion to something bigger than yourself.

Still, I wondered, what about the "real world"? What if you were the janitor in a school instead of a monk in a monastery? What if you worked behind a food counter or on a manufacturing line for minimum wage? What if you were that lawyer who despised her job and felt trapped by golden handcuffs? Or the caregiver obligated to serve an unbearably tough family member? What if your job was to spend all day calling strangers who didn't want to be bothered and asking them for money?

Our old friend Adam Grant got curious about this very question. He set his sights on employees at a public university's call center. This is a tough job. All day, every day, you cold call busy people who want nothing to do with you and ask for their time and money. The pay is low. The work is scripted and monotonous. Nearly everyone you speak with rejects you. Many of those respond with anything from irritation to outright vitriol. Emotionally, this is a job that can gut you fast, so turnover tends to be high and job satisfaction tends to be low. Grant wanted to see if he could transform that entire dynamic. He wanted to see if he could, without doing anything to change the job itself, alter the way people experienced it enough to make them happier doing it, and also a lot more effective at it. If he could, it was a win-win. Employees would contribute in a way that made them feel better and the university would get more money.

So what did he do? A simple intervention. He connected these employees to their bigger purpose. It only took five minutes, yet everything changed. Turns out these call-center employees were asking for money to fund student scholarships, but they'd never met anyone who had benefited from their work. Grant invited a group of scholarship recipients in to tell their stories to the call-center employees, to describe how the scholarships had made a real difference in their lives. The whole thing lasted just a few minutes, but the effect on the workers was profound. Now they weren't dialing just for dollars; they were dialing for living, breathing students they'd met in the flesh, whose lives they were capable of changing. What was once menial was now meaningful. Over the next month, the employees who had spent time with the true beneficiaries of their work spent twice as much time on the phone and raised more than twice as much scholarship money than those who hadn't met the scholarship students. This simple, five-minute intervention not only added a deeper sense of purpose, but also improved productivity and performance, heaping on the feel-good benefits of proficiency, progress, and accomplishment.

Researchers Amy Wrzesniewski, Justin Berg, and Jane Dutton found something similar. They looked at a hospital maintenance staff tasked with cleaning up after sick and deceased patients. Imagine what that might involve. Seriously, stop for a moment and think about it. That is a tough job, and the people who do it are often treated with anything from disdain to outright disrespect by both patients and staff. Yet many of them found great reward in their job by turning the *actual* job into something far beyond the job *description*. They would often respond to patient requests, spend time chatting with them, and go out of their way to help. They felt a genuine sense of concern and responsibility for the patients, almost like they were a part of the patient care team. By expanding the job "on paper" to incorporate what made them feel good, they were able to transcend the circumstance that would have otherwise left them empty.

I've bumped into this a bunch in the work we do at Good Life Project. Many folks come to us in the middle years of life bearing great responsibilities and feeling depleted by their work. They're often desperate to change positions or even entire careers and are looking for permission, then guidance. They've endured so much pain for so long, they don't want to hear anything but "Go for it, blow it up." Being a dad and husband myself, I can't be the rubber stamp they're looking for. In my experience, step one is not the nuclear job option. Step one is to do everything you can to make what you've got as good as it can get. If you've done that work and it's failed, then you look at more disruptive change. But that's not most people's truths.

In fact, it's often the opposite. There's this weird, counterintuitive thing we do when we're working at a life-sucking job. Instead of becoming aggressively proactive in the name of making it as good as we can, we get relentlessly good at making it as bad as we can. We often have no idea how complicit we've become, that we're actually a big part of the problem. Why do we do this? My guess is that it makes it easier to rationalize leaving and enduring the often immense pain of disruption that'll go along with a departure.

I'm not saying you should never leave a job that depletes you. I'm just saying you should own the truth of the situation first. Own your potential contribution to making it so bad (or not). Own the job of doing everything you can to make it as good as it can get. With rare exception, you'll find you can make nearly any job or task bearable, and many even beautiful. If, at that point, you still want to leave, you'll do it with far more conviction. And if the job that was depleting you is a role you cannot abandon because it's a responsibility you've undertaken as part of faith or family, you'll find yourself more easily able to experience it from a place of grace.

The big question, of course, is how do you do this? Part of it is counterintuitive. It comes from reclaiming a commitment to filling your Vitality Bucket. When your body and mind are tuned and optimized, everything gets better. The other part is to step back, look at your current gig, ask a few questions, and start making changes. The beautiful thing here is that it's often small changes that make the biggest, fastest difference. We saw that with Adam Grant's five-minute intervention. We saw it with the many momentary chats the hospital cleaning staff had with patients. Tiny tweaks often lead to big shifts. I'll share some questions to ask and areas to think about in today's exploration.

Daily Exploration:

Here are some questions to get you thinking about ways to either change what you experience or change the frame you bring to the experience, in order to find deeper fulfillment in the way you're contributing to the world:

1. *If I believed with every fiber of my being this was the work I had to do until the job was done, that there was no way out, no bigger, better deal, what might I do to make it as good as it could possibly get?* Note: If your answer is "nothing," and it comes in less than 10 seconds, it's almost a guaranteed self-lie designed to give you permission to leave. There is always at least one thing. When you think of that, it often triggers another, then another and another.

2. *What relationships might I work harder to build, mend, deepen, or expand that would allow me to experience this work with more ease, grace, confidence, strength, meaning, purpose, lightness, or joy?*

3. *What specific tasks and responsibilities would I give up, hand off, or do differently that would make a real difference in the way I experience this work? What new tasks and responsibilities might I take on?* Note: Counterintuitive as it sounds, taking on more of the "right" things can actually increase the sense of meaning and accomplishment, even if your job does not specifically require it.

4. *Is there a bigger purpose or community or person (or Divine source, however you might describe it) I am deeply connected to that the work I am doing is serving?*

5. *How might I build my nonwork life around what I do in a way that lets me frame it as a source of greater meaning, joy, connection, and engagement or something that gives me the freedom to do other things that provide those feelings?*

6. *Am I aggressively working to fill my Vitality Bucket every day?*

These aren't easy questions, but they're important ones. You may go through them and be able to say, with complete integrity, "I've done everything I can do. I'm good with the effort I've put in. It's time to move on." If so, do what you feel you need to do. If not, if your answer to the above questions leads to work still to be done, much as you might prefer to just move on, it's probably not yet time. First, make your chosen form of contribution as good as it can get. Then, if it's still not good enough, circle back to the many things you've learned about what matters (your spark, strengths, values, beliefs, and more), then begin to explore how you might leverage them better elsewhere.

DAY 10

think ripple, not WAVE

I've no idea how it happened, but it did. And man, am I glad.

It started as a simple blog post. Every January, I would reflect on the year behind me and set intentions for the year to come. A few thousand words in, I'd hit publish, and that would be that. Not this time.

My January 2012 post seemed to want to write itself longer. And longer, and longer. Until, a few maniacal weeks in, it had claimed 39 pages and a big, bold design and had become a Warren Buffett–style annual report. Along the way, I'd revealed things I had never written or spoken about, explored my work and where I was headed more transparently than ever before. Hitting publish made me nervous. Actually that's an understatement; it made me nauseous. Which is how I knew I had to do it.

The response to the report was stunning. It was a set of 10 simple ideas that I shared on the final two pages that created the biggest stir. Those 10 guiding principles, channeled through me in a matter of minutes, ended up becoming a catalyst for the next season of my career and life.

I called them, playfully, my "10 Commandments of Epic Business," and, having a little bit of self-mocking fun, I presented them in the voice of God with each line starting, "Thou shalt. . . ." Truth is, while couched as business principles, these 10 commandments were about something bigger. They were my guide on how to contribute to the world in a way that matters. How to build not just a good living, but a good life.

One of the commandments, "Thou shalt do epic shit," also garnered a bit more attention than some of the others. I wrote it this way because I was looking to provoke a conversation and also because I just thought it would be a fun, slightly edgy way to say, "Do stuff that matters." Since writing it, though, I've come to realize that its phrasing, without context or deeper explanation, may have caused as much harm as it did fun and good.

The problem with "Do epic shit" is that many people will read it as "If it's not epic, it's not worth doing." I'm not entirely opposed to that reading. Where things fall apart, though, is how so many people define the word *epic* in this context. To qualify as epic, they believe, you have to do something massive. You've got to create a huge wave that crashes on the beach and makes a giant splash. You have to go big and bold, do something that's risky and grand and matters to a lot of people. *Epic*, I've come to learn, is often translated as "extreme." Sometimes, doing epic things does mean big, bold, and extreme. But even more often, it's the exact opposite. Epic outcomes derive far more often from tiny, repeated, and deliberate drops of intention and action that ripple out in a quieter, gentler, yet equally expansive and impactful way. Epic is as much the ripple as it is the wave. But the way we talk about it, the way I'd framed it, implies the only way to live an epic life, to contribute meaningfully, to matter, is to go big.

Not only is that wrong, but for many it's crippling. The thought of going big often cultivates fear, paralysis, and disempowerment. We flog ourselves, thinking, "What if I fail in a big, public way?" For most people, the risk of a big, public failure and the judgment and loss that come with it is enough to keep them from even trying. So they give up on the entire notion of taking epic action, when, in truth, simply redefining epic action to include the ripple along with the wave gives a path for anyone to play big, to make a difference, one drop, one ripple at a time.

I started to realize that telling people to operate on the level of epic, without providing any further guidance, was doing more harm than good. It was shutting them down. tantamount to telling someone that, until they know their life purpose, everything they do is just killing time. I hate that proclamation, and there I was setting up so many for failure on a similar level.

What to do? I grappled with this for a long time. Do I lose the word *epic*? Nah. I still love the word. Well, what if I showed a different path? One that was more approachable to anyone? Not the wave, but the ripple.

In the middle of this exploration, an alert popped up on my screen. I know, I know, writing a book with Facebook open in the background, bad move. I'm still working on the whole attention thing. Wait, hold on. Okay, I'm back. That message was from a close friend and recent grad of our Good Life Project Immersion, an intimate and pretty intense retreat in Costa Rica.

On the final morning of that retreat, we awakened to a warm, tropical rain and made our way into the glass-walled practice room overlooking the entire San Jose Valley. A few years earlier, studying the intersection of Buddhism and the work of leading voices in the field of positive psychology, I had stumbled upon *metta*, or loving-kindness meditation. My friend and Shambhala Buddhist meditation teacher Susan Piver had taken me a bit deeper into the practice. The instructions were deceptively simple, but the experience was stunningly powerful in its ability to change states and cultivate connection and compassion, both toward yourself and others.

Sitting before the room of "GLeePers" who had just been through four powerful, vulnerable, and revealing days, I thought a guided *metta* meditation would be a nice way to close our time together. I took my seat and offered the simple repetition of phrases (a variation of the loving-kindness meditation language I shared in the "Cultivate Compassion" chapter). With the ethereal soundscape of the rain and the deep emotions that often arise during this practice, the room was transformed. While we'd all continue in the program together for months, I thought that simple moment had come to an end. *It was beautiful*, I thought, *but certainly not* epic. I couldn't have been more wrong. The first drop had hit the pond; the ripple had begun. But I wouldn't know it for another four months.

Jeffrey Davis, a soulful member of the family that had been birthed in Costa Rica, decided his experience with *metta* was a beginning and not an end. Here, with Jeffrey's permission, is what he shared with the entire group:

> Last night, I invite the 6-year-old into my study. Tell her I'd like to share something with her. Light candle. Sit cross-legged. Give her simplified version of JF's kindness meditation with our hands on our heart. She's reluctant. Then softens when she knows she can invite our dead cat Miklos into her heart. Softens more when I tell her I used to do something like this on my own as a boy to help me get to sleep. She giggles. We bow out.
>
> Tonight she comes to the study, sits on the floor: "Papa, can we invite some things into our heart tonight?"
>
> "Sure. Before or after stories?"
>
> "Before. I want to invite the sun and moon into my heart tonight."
>
> We practice. First with ourselves. She: "And you will say, 'Jeffrey, may you be happy.'"
>
> And then to our family and each other. And the cat. And the sun and moon and stars. And the world. And the candle. And the house. Because why not. It's all animate. It's all part and parcel of the same good stuff. Life. And it all merits kindness.

I read Jeffrey's words and nearly cried. At first because of the beautiful connection he has cultivated with his little girl and the love that seems to pour from her wise, connected take on the world at such a young age. But also because it gave me a profound new context for a path to impact. It validated the idea of one simple yet soulful action, one ripple as a path to epic action and expansive impact.

In that moment, I came to understand that we are all capable of contributing to the world in a way that makes a profound difference. A rare few go big. Make the big gesture. Take the big risk. Expose themselves on a grand scale. Create and then ride the big wave. But most of us, myself included, take a different yet equally valid path. It's the path of the ripple. Simple actions, moments, and experiences. Created, offered, and delivered with such a purity of intention and depth of integrity and clarity that they set in motion a ripple that, quietly, in its own way, in its own time, expands outward. Interacting with, touching, mattering to people we've never met in ways we never conceived.

That is the simple, elegant, yet exceedingly epic power and potential of the ripple. You are not excluded simply because you aren't willing to go big and risk crashing hard in public.

You can apply the idea of the ripple to the way you contribute to the world, whether it's your vocation, business, career, or just the thing you do on the side that serves as a source of meaning and joy and connection.

Embracing the ripple has been particularly freeing for me as a maker and entrepreneur. It gives me a way to think about growing income and impact while minimizing complexity. I tend to have this recurring delusion of grandeur. I see friends building big businesses and think, "Dude, I want to make *that!*" Which really translates to "I want to get all the glory of having created something big and cool." Then I remember, or more likely my wife gently guides me back to reality.

I've launched and run businesses with physical locations, overhead, inventory, employees, and complex systems. It's amazing, but every element adds complexity and the opportunity for things to fail. Some people are wired to love that. They thrive on the hustle, the breathless barrage of fires being lit and others in need of dousing. Not me.

Complexity is a leech on my soul. I want to do epic things. I want to "go big." I want to matter. But I also want to be able to breathe. And sleep. And allow as often as I incite. That's where the ripple comes in. It gives me a way of thinking about making meaning (and money—hey, I'm a realist) on the scale that supports my good life while keeping it simple. Instead of a company, I'll write a book or give a talk. Instead of a large organization, I'll license my ideas. Instead of having to be in the middle of everything, I'll surround myself with people who are natural-born complexity sponges.

Milton Glaser is a stunning example of this. Well into his eighties as I write this, he is arguably the most iconic designer alive. He created the most ripped-off logo in history ("I Heart NY"); cofounded *New York* magazine; crafted thousands of iconic brands, images, products, and experiences; and taught tens of thousands of students. You may not know his name if you are not in the world of design, but you know his work. Why is he a wonderful example of the ripple effect? Because, despite the impact he's had on the lives of literally millions, he's kept things relatively simple. Rather than build a giant agency, he's worked out of the same studio, with just a handful of staff, for decades. His great joy, he shared with me, he's known since he was six. To create beauty that is, in some way, in service of others. To learn and eventually teach along the way. So he's done just that. Instead of an organization, he creates a series of posters that inspire a generation. He creates a brand that defines an experience. He teaches a new generation to think differently and do work that matters. Drip. Drip. Drip. He long ago made the leap from epic to iconic.

Question is, how might you do the same?

Daily Exploration:

Think about the kind of work that sparks you. How might you pursue that work in a way that leads to meaningful outcomes but minimal complexity? What could you do that will give you the greatest reward *and* allow you to spend the greatest amount of time doing the parts that most light you up?

Make a list of three to five simple things you might do or create that could serve as a drop in a pond that might ripple out and make a difference without your having to be involved.

Bringing it Home

I think I love you.

At a minimum, I'm pretty sure I want to hug you.

No, really.

If you've made it this far and you're not my mother, father, sister, wife, kid, best friend, or on my payroll, either (a) you are incredibly gracious with your time, (b) you're one of those people who read the last chapter first (spoiler alert: unicorns conquer the world, Johnny Depp is president, and love reigns supreme), or (c) something about this book lit you up. It made you want to learn more, do more, be more, give more, live more. For the sake of preserving my fragile ego, I'm going to roll with option (c)!

Seriously, if you've made it here, something big just happened. Somewhere along the way, you got sparked! As an author and a teacher and, well, a human being who cares, that is everything I could ever hope for. And for you the reader, it's pretty powerful confirmation that you're ready to do the work needed to craft your own good life.

Before we come full circle, though, there are two things I want to touch on. You may have noticed, I didn't dwell on money or happiness in this book. How could I just ignore the two things people often associate most with living a good life? Simple. They matter, but not in the way you think and not as much as you think. Money and happiness are better explored, and more likely to arrive, as beneficent by-products than as front-and-center goals.

Let's take happiness. You may have heard that you can just choose happiness. Keep thinking happy thoughts and happiness will magically become your persistent state. Except, our brains don't really work that way. In between those happy thoughts is a little thing called reality. Deciding you want to be happy is Step 1. But deciding and repeating "I am happy" doesn't a happy person make. That's called being a Pollyanna. It's more about self-delusion than elevation. I can't tell you how many times I've seen crying eyes behind a pasted-on smile. In the end, it always melts away.

Real happiness comes not when you choose to be happy, but when you *discover the things that will make you happy and then do them.* What are those things? Pretty much all the things that fill your Good Life Buckets. Make good friends, do meaningful work, cultivate love and compassion, optimize your mind and body, step into your potential, dive into all the other things we've talked about, and guess what? Happiness ensues. Not because you said or thought you wanted to be happy, but because you built your life around people and pursuits that *made* you happy. Focus on the buckets and there's a pretty solid chance you'll find yourself awash in as much happiness as you're wired to receive.

What about money? It matters. But not the way you might think. If you're living in poverty and can't cover your basics, every dollar earned increases happiness and life satisfaction. Once your living expenses are comfortably covered, though, more money has little, if any, effect on happiness. Giving up time doing what you love with people you love or sacrificing your vitality in the name of money beyond what you need to live comfortably becomes largely indefensible. Though there may be a bit of a hitch in this.

As it turns out, while earning more than you need to cover the basics may not make you happier, spending money on the right things will. What are the right things? Think experiences, not stuff. If you spend your extra dough on experiences, like travel and adventure, and you bring along people you love to be with or serve others along the way, those experiences *may* make your life better. In that way, more money lets you have more of those experiences, and that *can* lead to a better life.

The reason I used the words *may* and *can*, though, is because what I've just said about money doesn't tell the whole story. It doesn't factor in what you'll have to sacrifice in the name of making the money needed to have those experiences. If you end up destroying your relationships with friends or family or letting your Vitality Bucket run dry in order to earn enough to travel more, the net effect may well be emptier buckets, even given what the experience of travel might add. Something to think about when choosing how hard to work, what you're willing to give up, and what you plan on buying.

Money, then, becomes a really slippery and often illusory measure of a life well lived. It's not well correlated with happiness, vitality, and connection once you have enough to be baseline okay. And like happiness, it's often better explored more as a by-product than as a direct pursuit.

That brings us back to the buckets. More precisely, your buckets. If you haven't already begun, it's time to move beyond reading and start *doing* this book. Time to stand up and say, "I choose me. This is the day I begin *my* Good Life Project! That's Step 1. If you want a little private accountability, head over to our online Good Life Project community and declare, "It's on! I'm starting *my* Good Life Project today."

Then think about two friends (could be more) who would really love and benefit from the ideas in this book *and* would be open to joining you in *doing* the book together, as accountability and celebration buddies. Why does this matter? One, because it's more fun and it turns your quest into an automatic Connection Bucket filler. Two, because there's a mountain of research that shows you'll stick with it longer and be far more successful when you do it with friends. So, do you have your two people in mind? Great. Now e-mail or call them, tell them, "It's our time," get them on board.

Next, revisit the buckets and take your snapshot, if you haven't already (get your buddies to do the same). You can use the quick version in the book or go deeper with our free online GoodLife360

Snapshot quiz at goodlifeproject.com/bookinsider. Share your snapshot with your buddies, talk about what you've learned, what was surprising, what you're satisfied with, and where you want to experience something better.

Here's where it gets real. Look at each bucket. Notice which is in most dire need of filling. Focus your energy on filling the bucket that is either emptiest or seems to be causing you the most immediate pain. If all buckets seem equally in need, then rotate around, filling a different one a little bit each day. Your quest is to come to a place where your buckets are all bubbling over. Where you're moving through each day feeling vital, energized, strong, alive, and at ease. You are contributing meaningfully to the world; leveraging your strengths, values, wisdom, and abilities to their fullest; doing only what truly matters. You are surrounded by people you love being with, embraced by love and a deep sense of understanding and belonging. You feel connected to people and source, however you define it.

If you really want to challenge yourself, treat this book as your Good Life Project 30-day Bucket Challenge. Do one chapter a day in the order that makes most sense, based on how full each bucket is. As you move from these first 30 days out into the rest of your life, revisit the activities in the book. Find the ones that made the biggest difference and, if you feel inclined, incorporate as many as you can into your days. Continue to build your mindfulness practice, continue to give, to align your actions with your now deeper understanding of who you are and what you most need. Along the way, there's a good chance something cool will start to happen. Ideas for other ways to fill each bucket will start to drop from the sky. You can try those ideas out after moving through the foundation ones in this book.

Think about retaking your snapshot once a month. Why? It will give you a new baseline to help you better understand where to focus your energies moving forward. Maybe you started with a full Vitality Bucket, but after a huge deadline and nonexistent self-care, that bucket is nearly empty. Your monthly snapshot will let you know before it runs dry.

Truth is, filling your buckets, living a good life, is constantly a moving target. There is no single day when you get to say, "I've made it; I don't have to do anything more." There is no *there* there. You will be filling your buckets until the day you leave this planet. That's okay. It's actually more than okay. It is a gift to know that the learning, the opportunity to always grow and connect, never caps out.

A good life is not a place at which you arrive, it is a lens through which you see and create your world. Viktor Frankl tells us in *Man's Search for Meaning* that "between stimulus and response, there is a space. In that space is our power to choose our response. In our response lies our growth and our freedom." And in that growth and freedom lies the heartbeat of a life well lived.

Question is, will you exercise this power?

Will you choose to create the life you dream of living?

If not now, when?

ENDNOTES

[1] Agnes de Mille, *Martha: The Life and Work of Martha Graham* (New York, NY: Random House, 1991), 264.

[2] www.dailymail.co.uk/sciencetech/article-2783677/How-YOU-look-phone-The-average-user-picks-device-1-500-times-day.htm

[3] http://onlinelibrary.wiley.com/doi/10.1111/1467-8624.7402008/abstract;jsessio nid=04CEB32B970BD7D9B7DA6E34EE304420.f04t03. See also http://sleep. tau.ac.il/articles/sleep%20res-ext%202003.pdf.

[4] K. Wahlstrom, B. Dretzke, M. Gordon, K. Peterson, K. Edwards, and J. Gdula, "Examining the Impact of Later School Start Times on the Health and Academic Performance of High School Students: A Multi-Site Study. Center for Applied Research and Educational Improvement," The University of Minnesota (2014).

[5] https://www.nhlbi.nih.gov/files/docs/public/sleep/healthy_sleep.pdf, pp19-20.

[6] www.ncbi.nlm.nih.gov/pmc/articles/PMC3433717/figure/F1

[7] T. A. Qehr, "In short photoperiods, human sleep is biphasic," *Journal of Sleep Research* 1: 103–107. (1992): doi: 10.1111/j.1365-2869.1992.tb00019.x

[8] https://www.youtube.com/watch?v=AdKUJxjn-R8&feature=youtu.be&t=16m20s

[9] Martin E. P. Seligman, *Flourish: A Visionary New Understanding of Happiness and Well-being* (New York, NY: Atria Books, 2012), 84.

[10] Sonja Lyubomirsky, *The How of Happiness: A New Approach to Getting the Life You Want* (New York, NY: Penguin Books, 2007), 96.

[11] Eva M. Selhub and Alan C. Logan, *Your Brain on Nature: The Science of Nature's Influence on Your Health, Happiness, and Vitality* (New York, NY: Collins, 2014), 18–19.

[12] Carol S. Dweck, *Mindset: The New Psychology of Success* (New York, NY: Ballantine Books, 2007), 7.

[13] http://www.edweek.org/ew/articles/2015/09/23/carol-dweck-revisits-the-growth-mindset.html

[14] https://sivers.org/relax

[15] http://www.verizonwireless.com/news/article/2015/06/how-people-really-use-their-mobile-devices.html

[16] http://emergingtech.tbr.edu/news/smartphone-user-survey-glimpse-mobile-lives-college-students-0

[17] Arthur Aron, *Personality and Social Psychology Bulletin* Vol. 23 No. 4 (1997): 363–377.

[18] http://www.nytimes.com/2015/01/11/fashion/modern-love-to-fall-in-love-with-anyone-do-this.html

[19] Helen Fisher, *Why We Love: The Nature and Chemistry of Romantic Love* (New York, NY: Holt, 2004).

[20] Gary Chapman, *The Five Love Languages: How to Express Heartfelt Commitment to Your Mate* (Chicago, IL: Northfield, 2004), 10.

[21] http://www.bbc.co.uk/programmes/p018dvyg

[22] www.viacharacter.org/www/Research

[23] www.viacharacter.org/www/The-Survey#nav

[24] Danielle LaPorte, *The Desire Map: A Guide to Creating Goals with Soul* (Louisville, CO: Sounds True, 2014).

[25] Gabriele Oettingen, *Rethinking Positive Thinking: Inside the New Science of Motivation* (New York, NY: Current, 2014), 133.

[26] Stephen Post and Jill Neimark, *Why Good Things Happen to Good People: How to Live a Longer, Healthier, Happier Life by the Simple Act of Giving* (New York, NY: Broadway Books, 2008).

[27] Adam Grant, *Give and Take: A Revolutionary Approach to Success* (New York, NY: Viking, 2013).

[28] Viktor E. Frankl, *Man's Search for Meaning* (Boston, MA: Beacon Press, 2006).

A PERSONAL
INVITATION
FROM JONATHAN

Hey there (yup, you!),

First, thank you. No, really. Thank you. For reading this book. But also just for being so awesome (trust me, you are, I know . . . I've been watching! lol).

We need more of you in the world. People who are willing to step out of the "gray twilight," shake off the suffocating weight of "Reactive Life Syndrome," and step into a deeply connected, profoundly meaningful, and vital life.

And here's the thing. I could really use your help.

I'm growing a movement of lit-up humans. And this book, well, it's the kindling that lights the fire. The more it spreads, the more people we inspire, the bigger our family becomes, the better our lives get, starting with yours. So this is really hard to do. I'm still pretty uncomfortable with the whole vulnerability thing. But here goes.

Would you join this movement and help me grow it? Yes?! Oh, that's so fantastic!

Just take one simple step . . .

Join the Good Life Project Collective at:

GoodLifeProject.com/community

It's our private online and on-the-ground community, populated by awesome humans who see the world the way you do. We're a global bunch so you'll get to meet people from all over the world and maybe even find (or even start) a small group to meet up with in real life. Oh, and by the way, in case you're wondering, it's totally free!

Then if you're inclined, share this book. Lend your copy to a friend or give a copy (or two) as a gift so you can all "do the book" together. Whatever works best for you.

No more autopilot life. No more being asleep at the wheel. It's time for us all to rise together. To make the journey from flatlined to flourishing. To step back into our good lives and bring those we care about along with us!

With a whole lotta love & gratitude,

Jonathan

ACKNOWLEDGMENTS

Here's where I'm supposed to share how much effort goes into writing a book. Having crafted three different versions along the road to the one you're now reading, I was compelled to share Hemingway's famed line, "There is nothing to writing. All you do is sit down at a typewriter and bleed."

Here is the truth. Writing is hard. But to be in a place that allows the indulgence of time, space, and stillness needed to bring something like this to life, that, my friend, is a straight-up gift. There is no other lens. The book that has emerged is crafted not just by the hands of a single writer, alone in a room, but by a family of makers.

I am grateful to have been guided by the kindness and wisdom of my editor and linguistic soul-sister, Patty Gift, along with the contributions of Joan Oliver. The whole team at Hay House has been a joy to work with.

Thanks to Caroline Kelso Winegeart, who created a cover, interior illustrations, and lettering that helped add the element of visual delight. And to my agent, Wendy Sherman, for her contin-ued guidance along this journey between the pages.

To my Good Life Project family, what an incredible jaunt it's been, eternal gratitude for what you allow me to do, and who you allow me to be.

To my partner in life and business, Stephanie, how can I ever begin to describe the gift you've been to my every breath, every moment, every flutter of my heart. And to my kiddo, Jesse, you inspire me to no end. Thank you both for bearing with endless nights on the couch as I wrote madly to deadline, and for the bottomless well of hugs and kisses. There are no words, only love.

To my community of friends, colleagues, and co-conspirators in the adventure of life, you guys rock on every level!

To you, my kind reader, who holds this book in your hands, thank you. For your willingness to set aside your precious time and for your openness to exploring and sharing these words and ideas.

ABOUT THE AUTHOR

Jonathan Fields is a New York City dad, husband, award-winning author, teacher, speaker, media producer, and entrepreneur. His book *Uncertainty: Turning Fear and Doubt into Fuel for Brilliance* was named the top personal development book in 2011 by 800-CEO-READ. Jonathan's current focus, Good Life Project® (GLP), is a media and education venture and global movement that empowers people to live more meaningful, connected, and vital lives. The GLP podcast and video channels reach over 500,000 people a month in more than 150 countries with millions of views and listens, and its courses and events draw participants from around the world. You can visit Jonathan online at jonathanfields. com, discover GLP's podcast and video content and join the community at goodlifeproject.

Hay House Titles of Related Interest

YOU CAN HEAL YOUR LIFE, the movie, starring Louise Hay & Friends
(available as a 1-DVD program and an expanded 2-DVD set)
Watch the trailer at: www.LouiseHayMovie.com

THE SHIFT, the movie, starring Dr. Wayne W. Dyer
(available as a 1-DVD program and an expanded 2-DVD set)
Watch the trailer at: www.DyerMovie.com

◎ ◎ ◎

All of the above are available at your local bookstore,
or may be ordered by contacting Hay House (see next page).

◎ ◎ ◎

We hope you enjoyed this Hay House book. If you'd like to receive our online catalog featuring additional information on Hay House books and products, or if you'd like to find out more about the Hay Foundation, please contact:

Hay House, Inc., P.O. Box 5100, Carlsbad, CA 92018-5100
(760) 431-7695 or (800) 654-5126
(760) 431-6948 (fax) or (800) 650-5115 (fax)
www.hayhouse.com® • www.hayfoundation.org

◎ ◎ ◎

Published and distributed in Australia by: Hay House Australia Pty. Ltd., 18/36 Ralph St., Alexandria NSW 2015 • *Phone:* 612-9669-4299 • *Fax:* 612-9669-4144 www.hayhouse.com.au

Published and distributed in the United Kingdom by: Hay House UK, Ltd., Astley House, 33 Notting Hill Gate, London W11 3JQ • *Phone:* 44-20-3675-2450 *Fax:* 44-20-3675-2451 • www.hayhouse.co.uk

Published and distributed in the Republic of South Africa by: Hay House SA (Pty), Ltd., P.O. Box 990, Witkoppen 2068 • info@hayhouse.co.za_ www.hayhouse.co.za

Published in India by: Hay House Publishers India, Muskaan Complex, Plot No. 3, B-2, Vasant Kunj, New Delhi 110 070 • *Phone:* 91-11-4176-1620 *Fax:* 91-11-4176-1630 • www.hayhouse.co.in

Distributed in Canada by: Raincoast Books, 2440 Viking Way, Richmond, B.C. V6V 1N2 • *Phone:* 1-800-663-5714 • *Fax:* 1-800-565-3770 • www.raincoast.com

◎ ◎ ◎

<u>**Take Your Soul on a Vacation**</u>

Visit www.HealYourLife.com® to regroup, recharge, and reconnect with your own magnificence.Featuring blogs, mind-body-spirit news, and life-changing wisdom from Louise Hay and friends.

Visit www.HealYourLife.com today!